THE 50+
BOOMER

THE 50+ BOOMER

Your Key to 76 Million Consumers

by

Donald L. Potter

Gabriel Publications

Published by:
Gabriel Publications
14340 Addison St. #101
Sherman Oaks, California 91423
(818) 906-2147 Voice
(818) 990-8631 Fax
www.GabrielBooks.com

Copyright © 2002 by Donald L. Potter
ISBN 1891689-84-3
Library of Congress Catalog Card Number: 2002103726

Distributed by: Partners Book Distributors
Publisher: Rennie Gabriel
Cover illustration by Ramon Mediavillo
Typography: Synergistic Data Systems, sdsdesign@gte.net
Cover Design: Dale Schroeder, SDS

Manufactured in the United States of America

This book is dedicated to the most important people in my life:
My loving and supportive wife, Sue—the consummate Cutting-Edge Boomer;
my parents, Howard and Helen, who instilled me with values and a sense of morality that have helped shape my view of life;
my children, Hilary, Rachel and Adam, who continue to keep me from thinking and acting too old;
my granddaughter, Ashley, and the new grandchild on the way, who symbolize how important it is to encourage youngsters to learn, grow and live.

CONTENTS

Chapter 6

Chapter 7

Chapter 8

Chapter 9

Chapter 10

Chapter 11

Chapter 12

Chapter 13

ACKNOWLEDGMENTS

There are just too many individuals who have had an impact on the development of this book to list them all here. However, I would like to thank all those who led me to better understand and ultimately embrace the importance of the Cutting-Edge Boomers as possibly the most powerful consumer group on the face of the earth.

I do owe some special thanks to the following people: Dan Katz, who convinced me that the cemetery business actually offered our agency an interesting opportunity to learn more about marketing to an older audience; Ray Frew, who introduced me to many people who were targeting the 50+ consumer thus leading me to re-examine the dynamics of this growing market segment; Gary O'Sullivan, who inspired me to stick with the goal of finishing this text once I began the process; and Des Towey for his continued spiritual guidance and friendship. Additionally, my thanks goes to those who were directly involved in getting this book into its final form: Donatella Zerial for typing and retyping the manuscript until it was ready to submit; Tamara Podell for sourcing and researching much of the information required to produce this document; Robert Sax for his editorial and organizational insights; Ramon Mediavillo for creating the front cover design and illustration; Renee Ergazos who displayed great patience and professionalism in editing the book; and Rennie Gabriel for his publishing skills, which resulted in bringing this project to completion.

About the Author

Don Potter has more than 35 years of experience in advertising, sales and marketing. He has run a marketing consulting company and held top-level executive positions with leading advertising agencies. As an advertising executive, he was responsible for a number of award-winning campaigns. Mr. Potter has handled many well-known brands such as Alcoa, Clorox, Rockwell, Sunkist, Toyota and Weyerhaeuser.

Don Potter is an expert in packaged goods. He has owned his own food brokerage firm and held key sales and product management positions with several national grocery marketers. Among the many grocery firms Don Potter has served are Continental Baking, General Foods, H. J. Heinz, House Foods, Lever Bros., Nissin Foods, Pepperidge Farm, Sapporo Beer, Scott Paper, Stagg Foods and Western Bagel.

Don Potter is president and CEO of Potter, Katz, Postal & Ferguson, Inc. (PKPF), a full-service advertising, marketing and media-buying firm located in the NoHo Arts District of Los Angeles. Some of the agency's clients are Hitachi, The Catholic Cemeteries of the Archdiocese of Los Angeles, Hollywood Celebrity Diet, Kimlan Foods, Mount Sinai Memorial Parks and Mortuaries, New Balance, the Salvation Army and Vivitar. Mr. Potter writes frequently about marketing and advertising issues. He has also lectured at many conventions, seminars and leading universities including USC, UCLA, and Cal Poly.

Introduction

The Baby Boomers' rise to glory has been no real surprise because they represent the largest, most influential and affluent group of consumers in history. The first wave of Boomers has been the one to set the direction, style and tone for those who will follow. The 50+ Boomers, also known as Cutting-Edge Boomers, have made more of an impact on the way America, and the world, does business than any group before them. They have dictated the products we produce, the services we sell and the very nature of advertising.

In this book, we will focus on the 50+ Boomers because, like Slick Willie Sutton replied when asked why he robbed banks, "That's where the money is." For many goods and services, the Cutting-Edge Boomers are vital because that's where the money is. Those under 50 years of age often have different needs and wants; however, as they reach the half-century mark, you can expect them to behave much in the same way as their older brothers and sisters. Even if the Trailing Boomers are not of immediate importance, what one learns from the 50+ Boomers can be applied to the younger group in time.

The Pre-Boomers—those born before 1946 and under 65 years of age—are in many ways an extension of the 50+ Boomers because this slightly older group was influenced by many of the same events. According to the U.S. Census Bureau (2000), the combined 50 to 64 age group is comprised of over 40 million consumers. This group is too large and too wealthy to overlook. However, we will concentrate on marketing considerations for the 50+

Boomer, knowing that efforts aimed at them will naturally affect the purchasing patterns of likeminded consumers, even if they are slightly younger or older.

Marketers allocate big budgets to establish their products and services early in the formative years of the consumer's buying cycle and continue to fight for this presence during the heavy usage periods in the following years. That's why people in the age group of 18 to 49 have the unwavering attention of most advertisers and their agencies. For years, the people making decisions at these companies had fallen into this age group themselves, and mass media made it easier and more profitable to direct most of their marketing money toward this large group of free thinking, free spending consumers known as the Baby Boomers. But something's happening along the way, the Boomers are getting older. People born between 1946 and 1964 are classified as the Baby Boomer generation, and all 76 million of them are doing what generation after generation has done since the beginning of time; they're aging. But they are not aging like their parents did, nor anyone who preceded them. This army of true consumers, the first wave of which already turned 55 last year, doesn't think, doesn't feel and doesn't act like the middle-age groups that preceded them.

Unlike their parents' generation, there was not a Depression to curb their spending habits and establish their need for security. They were not part of the World War II effort to defend freedom; they were only a byproduct of its aftermath. They did not cause the post-war growth, but they did taste its fruits. They grew up, for better or worse, in the era of television, sex, drugs, and rock 'n roll, and many had an acute distrust of authority plus an overwhelming feeling of entitlement. The "I want it all and I want it now" attitude created another label for the Boomer generation—the "Me" generation.

Getting older has not necessarily been easy for the Boomers. They scoffed at the white-bread TV shows that many of them grew up with, *Father Knows Best, Leave it to Beaver* and *The Partridge Family*; accordingly, they created their own version of family values. Typically, the modern Boomer household is hard working (husband and wife hold down full-time jobs), free spending (put it on the credit card) trying to raise a family, and seeking some semblance of normal life in this fast changing world in which we live.

Whatever they've done, good and bad, the first wave of Boomers has always set the direction, the style and the tone for those who will follow—including their children and their children's children. No other group has been as influential on the way we do business than the Cutting-Edge Boomers. Yet something seems terribly wrong. Are these once vital consumers being replaced by another, more viable group? Have they become a less valuable target audience? Should the Boomers move on and make room for the X, Y and Z generations?

To some, the answer appears to be a simple "yes." I say it is a definite "no!" Why the disparity? Look at the make-up of the marketing departments of most consumer products and service companies as well as their agency counterparts. What do you see? Are most of the brand managers and account people under the age of 35? Does it take a lot of searching to find someone over 40 working the front lines at an ad agency? Yet those under 40, even under 30, are the people who are developing the strategies, creating the ads and determining what media will carry the messages. Are they ignoring the goose that laid the golden egg, or just catering to the next logical power base of new consumers?

After all, times change as do consumers, and the way marketers communicate evolves along with them. In my 40 years in the marketing and advertising business, I've seen change happen many times. Being born ahead of the Boomers, I was able to observe and evaluate what actually happened as the Boomers reached their milestones. I have studied how advertisers have treated the aging process, and it has been a fascinating education. As a result, I am an advocate for marketing to the 50+ consumer and hope in some way to become a "pied piper" for both the consumer as well as interested marketers.

Understanding the maturation process of this group, embracing the implications and utilizing this information properly can open up an entirely new potential for curious marketers, rather than close the door on old friends. The Radio Advertising Bureau (January, 2002) reported to their members that the 50–55 age cell has been the fastest growing segment over the past decade. In this same report, they stated that advertisers are designating less than 5 percent of their total advertising dollars to this demographic. It is now time for marketers to recognize the importance of this maturing consumer.

Chapter 1

Fifteen Things Every Marketer Should Know About the 50+ Boomers

Before sorting out the specifics of reaching these Cutting-Edge Boomers, and those who directly preceded them or are soon to join their ranks, there are a number of considerations that must be addressed. What I'm suggesting is that unless you and I concur on these core beliefs, the discussion that follows will not have much meaning to you; therefore, you probably will not act on these suggestions. However, if you find yourself agreeing, read on and discover more about the world of "Second Half Marketing.™" As a starting point, let's look at fifteen things every marketer should know about the 50+ market.

1. **Boomers Are Redefining what "Old" Means.**

   Being old used to mean reaching the half-century mark. The first wave of Boomers are already past this formerly magic number, and reaching old age is becoming a more distant event. Now it has moved past 60, past 65 to 70 and older. To see how far this perceived age-line is pushed into the future, we must keep track of the Boomers as the years go by to see how old they must be before they start to *act* old.

2. They Are Better Prospects than the 50+ People of the Past.

The Cutting-Edge Boomers have money, are willing to spend it, and seem to be prepared to consume for years to come. There are more of them in raw numbers—twice as many people as the previous generation—yet they cannot be defined by demographics alone. The real success will be through a targeted marketing approach that addresses their psychographic differences and celebrates their lifestyles.

3. The 50+ Boomers Need More Nurturing.

Turning 50 is a big deal for the youth-obsessed Boomers, even if most treat it as just another birthday. Inside, they are beginning to realize they have reached the time when things will change more quickly, fewer years lie ahead than behind them, and their priorities will be different than in the past. This self-realization becomes clearer as the years pass. If your advertising does not reflect an understanding of this phenomenon, you may not be communicating with them effectively.

4. Children of 50+ Boomers Don't Know How to Sell to Their Parents.

The 50+ Boomers think young, but you can't treat them like kids. In-your-face ads, computer-generated graphics, hip and irreverent copy may cause the under-35 age groups to act, but these messages tend to turn off older consumers. Young ad people naturally feel most comfortable, and are probably most effective communicating, with their peers rather than learning what motivates an older generation.

5. 50+ Consumers Are Not Necessarily Blindly Brand Loyal.

They certainly have more experience in making buying decisions, so if a brand does not appear to understand their perceived needs or assaults them with ads that insult their sensitivities or, maybe worse yet, ignores them altogether, chances are there is a brand switch in the making. Do not take them for granted.

6. 50+ Boomers Without Children Living at Home Are Still an Important Market.

Certainly, consumable products need to continue to appeal to these Empty-Nesters. After all, the companies selling these products have invested too much over the years to risk letting a competitor steal the market away. Consider durables. Cutting-Edge Boomers have homes and buy appliances, TVs, and cars. They also remodel, redecorate, and replace a lot of things. Although they are not slaves to fashion, and do not spend most of their disposable income on clothes and accessories, they continue to be a major market force here too. Unlike their younger counterparts, you can look to the Cutting-Edge Boomers to stick with trends rather than start or latch on to fads. The beauty of this concept is that trends last while fads don't.

7. The 50+ Consumer Spends More Money on Everything They Used to Buy.

There really is a life for mom and dad after putting the children through college and this means spending more on themselves. Empty-Nesters are estimated to have $5000 to $10,000 more annually in disposable income to spend once the children leave home. Remember that they are the "Me" generation. They're spending on entertainment, both in and outside the home, leisure activities, travel, personal toys and now everything that grandparents buy. This is a huge emerging market.

8. 50+ Boomers Are Helping Their Parents Make Decisions.

Modern medicine has extended life and, in many instances, has improved the quality of the golden years. Many of the Boomers are, or will be, responsible for their parents' well-being in the years ahead. If not financially, at least they will provide emotional support. They will be key influencers in many decisions ranging from investments to healthcare, housing to recreation, and nutrition to final arrangements. While they are dealing with these areas for their parents, they will be gathering information and forming perceptions, which later they will use to make many of the same decisions for themselves.

9. Staying in Shape and Maintaining Good Health Is an Obsession with Many 50+ Boomers.

Many are engaged in regular exercise, while others are ready to try the latest diet plan or product. More Boomers eat healthier than they once did and have added vitamins and supplements to their daily intake. These regimens, along with the collateral products and services, offer great marketing opportunities. Don't forget about the "nip here and tuck there" potential for the "look young at any cost" segment of the aging market. This applies to both men and women, so look for pills, lotions and potions, as well as elective surgeries to grow in popularity.

10. 50+ Boomers Are Becoming More Skeptical as They Grow Older.

Life may not have delivered all that was promised or due to them, but they are not ready to give up. They will keep on working because the 50+ Boomers are not content nor resigned to live as their parents' generation had. They still want it all, but don't quite know how to get it. Even those who are better off financially seem to have questions. The marketer who will succeed is the marketer who knows how to approach this skepticism and provides answers to the consumer through the appropriate products and services or, at a minimum, considers these feelings in the way advertising is directed to this audience.

11. Those 50+ Cannot Be Lumped into a Big, Evolving, Homogeneous Group for Marketing Purposes.

As people in past generations grew older, they seemed to become more alike in their preferences. The Cutting-Edge Boomers are still a diverse group with many different interests and a variety of lifestyles. It is too soon to tell how and when the Boomers will come together, if at all. Will the catalyst be the natural progression of aging, or will some major galvanizing event be the trigger? The tragedy of September 11, 2001 gave us a glimpse of how Americans can unite. Only time will tell how the Cutting-Edge group will behave in the years ahead. This behavior will affect how you will communicate with them.

12. 50+ Boomers Will Not Be Denied Their Power.

It is vital to spot the developing trends. After all, the total Boomer population is greater than the nation's three largest states (California, New York, and Texas) combined—that's clout. But these people do not just reside in a few states; they are spread all over this great nation. And they have varying needs, which must be identified and met if you want their business once they turn 50.

13. The 50+ Boomers' Politics Have Changed Somewhat, but the Swing Has Not Been as Much to the Right as with Older Generations.

These people, for the most part, gravitated from a farther left position, many with their social conscience being akin to religious fervor. Most have lost this activist commitment, becoming more fiscally conservative while holding on to what they believe is their social responsibility. Some have even made the journey back to an organized religion, while others are still searching for something more important than themselves.

14. All the Acronyms of the Late 1980s Are the Cutting-Edge Boomers of Today.

The Yuppies (young urban professionals) and DINKs (dual income no kids), as well as college protesters, Vietnam Vets and other such groups have grown up to be 50+ as well. Although they've matured, the Cutting-Edge Boomers tend to have fond memories of their youth, but they are not looking back. The Cutting-Edge Boomer will influence the Trailing Boomer's behaviors and preferences just as they have been over the years.

15. 50+ Boomers Offer the Greatest, Immediate Opportunity to Increase the Effectiveness of Your Internet Marketing Efforts.

Whether the strategy is to bring them to your website, provide them with information, and capture their names for future use, or to make an online sale right now; these people can mean the difference between profit and loss. Although many are not as proficient with computers as younger people are, most Boomers learned the fundamentals in order to survive in the work force. The interesting aspect of this is that they don't spend as much time in front of the computer as younger people. Boomers use the computer to help them make more informed decisions and for more convenient communicating. However, you still must use traditional media, in addition to search engines, to drive them to your site.

Having pondered the above points, did you discover areas that your marketing efforts have not yet considered? Is the 50+ Boomer an untapped, unexplored or underdeveloped marketing opportunity awaiting your attention? If you are ready to dig deeper, read on and we will define this potential more fully.

Chapter 2

THE 50+ BOOMERS ARE NOT THEIR PARENTS' GENERATION

Selling to the 50+ Boomers isn't different from the efforts required to influence other consumers. However, knowing what drives these Cutting-Edge Boomers is the secret to success.

The foundation of the pitch, be it one-on-one or through mass media, is to understand as much as possible about the prospect: their needs and wants, their likes and dislikes, their hot buttons and turn-offs. Determining what makes them act the way they do, and how you can make them think differently regarding a particular product or service, is key. Much of this information has already been quantified in secondary research, such as magazine and industry surveys, but more data is waiting to be extrapolated. Much can be learned through observation. Of course primary research can always be instituted in order to pinpoint attitudes and confirm psychographic considerations. You can never know too much about your prospect.

What makes the Cutting-Edge Boomers different from the age groups that bookend them—those over 55, and those younger than 50? And just as important, what are the similarities?

An Emerging Profile

Many of the Cutting-Edge Boomers were the ones with the idealistic personality types—the dreamers. As they matured, reality set in and they became more adaptive. Early on, they envisioned a world at peace and a world of equality. Years of working to keep their personal hopes alive eventually brought their activism closer to home; to their own families and communities. As a result, it became more important to learn how to be part of the World Wide Web than to get involved in worldwide issues. This does not suggest that these Boomers have lost their hearts, as much as it indicates that with age they have also learned to use their heads.

It was just a matter of time before much of the "Me" generation would be forced to deal with the pragmatism of individual responsibilities and let go of some of the altruistic concerns of their youth. Job and family issues moved to the forefront of their personal agendas. Some remain vocal about things such as the environment, human rights and gun control, but many are only politically involved on Election Day. "Cause-marketing" efforts and certain charitable organizations appeal to the 50+ Boomers' hearts and, therefore, have a great opportunity for enticing this market segment to donate time or money to worthwhile projects.

These Boomers still have a sense of entitlement, although it's not as overwhelming as it once was. Most have worked hard for what they've achieved. Better education and this country's economic prosperity have placed many Cutting-Edge Boomers in a better financial position than their parents or even their older brothers and sisters. Additionally, having a several-year head start over those who are following them, the 50+ group feels pretty positive about who they are and what they've accomplished.

Nonetheless, they don't have delusions of grandeur about the future. They realize that if they haven't reached their business and financial goals set many years ago, they're probably not going to achieve them. There's a little twinge of disappointment, but this is countered by life being good overall. Although they don't have everything they want, most of the 50+ Boomers have what they need. The trick now is to figure out what has to be done to maintain this good lifestyle.

Playing Catch-Up

Planning for the future was not one of the Cutting-Edge Boomer's strengths. They always believed they could make more money; therefore, they spent it as they made it. Somehow they got through the difficult years with some money in the bank, some debts to pay and a chance to save for retirement. However, retirement seems to become more and more distant. Most 50+ Boomers are not going to be in a position to retire at 65. In fact, the notion of retirement is being pushed farther and farther into the future. Many believe they'll never fully retire. That means financial services are something of acute interest to these Cutting-Edge Boomers. This also suggests that they will be full-blown consumers for many years to come. If they don't retire or delay it indefinitely, look to these Boomers to keep consuming as long as they're working, even if it's only part-time. This kind of thinking got them into this predicament in the first place, but nobody is going to change this attitude at this stage of the game.

For those men and women who can slow down a bit, hobbies will play a more important role in their lives. Nostalgia from their childhood, including collectables, will also get considerable attention. This opens up an array of new marketing possibilities.

Having the opportunity to be better educated than previous generations has not necessarily resulted in this group becoming more intellectually curious. Some were pampered, while at the same time, being neglected. Many of their mothers worked, and life for their parents became busier as the need to create a stronger financial foundation emerged after World War II. And of course, TV became a central part of the children's lives. With this came less reading and more TV watching. Kids didn't have to think because the tube did it for them. There was less need to dig for information because someone else was doing it. Superficial characters on TV extended to a society that didn't have a great deal of depth in the first place. Many who grew up during this formative period often lived on or near the surface, carrying the attitude, "As long as I get what I want, there's no problem."

The civil rights movement, coupled with the Vietnam War and women's rights, came to the forefront as a result of TV reporting. What had been someone else's isolated issue suddenly was propelled live into our living rooms. Young people at the time were appalled by man's inhumanity to man. They could relate to one cause, or maybe all of them, and they believed it was time to do something about it.

After all, civil rights was the first cousin of women's rights. The anti-war protesters were about everyone's rights, and these protesters thought government was the culprit in the center of it all. It was time for the young people to unite and be heard, and they did just that. America's youth used these talking points as the reason to shout in rebellion, not just against perceived injustices but against the very traditions and values they were brought up with. The media loved it, the protesters pushed forward, and parents, on an individual basis, could do little to stop the ground swell. To many of the older generations, the moral fiber of this country was being destroyed by those who would someday have to stitch it back together. It was a turning point, a space in time that would forever change the way Americans thought and acted.

Now the baton is passing hands, the older generation is dying at an increasing rate. Soon the aging Boomers will take the place of their parents and become the older generation, but the passage won't be an easy one. They're not about to act or think old, nor are they prepared to become the kind of authority figures their parents were accused of being. Boomers generally prefer the "live and let live" attitude; they would rather be friends with their children and allow them to do their own thing than have to act like a parent. There could be considerable marketing implications and far-reaching political impact if the Cutting-Edge Boomers begin to take a stronger stand on social and personal issues with their coming of age.

Changes Over Time

Sooner or later Boomers will have to grow up. In the meantime, their thinking makes self-help and group therapy a big business. Even the fitness trend is based on looking good and feeling good. And speaking about looking good, industry research indicates that women over 50 account for nearly three times more clothing sales than their population numbers would suggest (U.S. Bureau of Labor Statistics, Consumer Expenditure Survey, 1997). They are also becoming grandmothers in greater numbers. These women are the driving force behind the marked increase in cosmetic surgery. So any product or service that suggests there's a "fountain of youth" at the end of the rainbow has a ready and willing market. Because their internal time clock is ticking, they must act now to ward off the effects of aging. Many will spend significant dollars in an attempt to maintain their youth, even though they can't stop the inevitable.

Accepting the passage of time as just being part of life will occur as these Boomers pass the mid-50s mark. It's uncharted territory, but they're arriving in droves; one every 8 seconds or so will reach this magic age of 50 for the next 20 years according to the *AdWeek* Demographic Report, May 10, 1999. A successful marketer will be one who gives them a helping hand: first to pass through the portal of time into the second half, and then through the early part of this new life experience. Help them accept this change now, and stay with them in the years that follow. What do you have to offer these new pioneers? How will you help them become settlers in their new life?

Those marketers who wish to pursue this growing consumer group must provide the products and services that satisfy the changes occurring in the 50+ Boomers' lifestyles. Educating them about products will require more than a features-and-benefits story. It will take a demonstrative effort to earn their trust by showing a true understanding of their transitioning needs and desires. There is no substitute for being able to relate, by having either "walked in their shoes" or at least knowing the path that these consumers are following.

Chapter 3

WHAT THE 50+ BOOMERS FEAR

There are two basic fears that I believe the 50+ Boomers must face as part of their passage to the next level in the continuum of life. These are not related to survival or any of the creature comforts both sexes need and want. One is male oriented, the other is more likely to affect women. These fears are a powerful influence in the Cutting-Edge Boomer's lives as they deal with the aging process. *Men fear losing power and women fear becoming invisible.*

As you ponder this statement, you may well arrive at the same conclusion I did. These are not two separate issues; rather they are simply different sides of the same coin. What we're really dealing with is *control.*

It's Hard to Give Up the Reins

For many men, lack of power is their dilemma. Even those who currently hold powerful positions know that one day they will have to step down and turn the controls over to someone else—someone younger. Look at Jack Welch, the CEO of General Electric (G.E.) who retired at the age of 65 in September of 2001. He made G.E. the most valuable company in the world during his 20 year run as the CEO. Arguably, Welch is the best CEO of our times. Yet he could not go quietly, even after his spectacular run of taking a company that had a market capital of 13 billion to over $400 billion during a two-decade period. He delivered consistently high profits and diversified the company so that G.E. is positioned to continue its winning ways for many years to come. In his final six months, Mr. Welch attempted to engineer a takeover of Honeywell, another global giant. He wanted to go out in a blaze of glory. Instead, his aggressiveness angered the European Common Market members and they rejected the merger. Although embarrassing, this does not lessen the outstanding achievements of Mr. Welch. However, it makes you wonder if this was just a high-powered CEO pushing ahead until the very end, or someone who didn't want to let go and tried to ease the pain of the ultimate loss of power by orchestrating his last hurrah.

Most men aren't in such high profile positions, so they tend to slip into losing their power in much quieter, but nonetheless just as devastating, scenarios. Mr. Welch was 65 and the Cutting-Edge Boomers are younger by ten years or more, so they won't have to face this kind of trauma for some time. After all, isn't this more of a retirement crisis than anything else? I don't think so. Even though most men don't give much thought to being 50 until they reach 55, it appears that their inner radar picks up on events that could affect them in the future.

I talked with a number of men (especially men over 50) about the last days of Jack Welch at G.E. They seemed to concur that the deal itself was probably more important than the need for the merger and question the timing for the transaction. Those in business, who held management positions, or who had a driven personality, understood the burning desire to pull off one last and biggest ever deal. Others didn't identify as readily. However, people I spoke with who were nearer to retirement actually related to this matter as if they were walking in Mr. Welch's shoes. They had followed the news and understood why this was the most important thing to accomplish before "being put out to pasture."

The point is this: men who never wanted to admit their mortality don't do so until they lose a parent or a friend their own age. The same kind of false bravado applies to vulnerability. Men give some thought to it because women have told us we must become more compassionate. Aside from reactions to the personal loss of a loved one or sadness expressed towards a major tragedy, men don't like to cry in public or allow emotions to bubble to the surface. Many of these men fought in Vietnam or lost friends in the war, but their outward reactions were more of anger than sadness. Sometimes an emotional display is permissible, like when watching a sports movie alone. But, if men have been like this all their lives, why should anyone expect them to suddenly open up once they reach 50?

It won't happen. In fact, chances are these 50+ Boomer men will avoid subjects about control. In their minds, not facing it is synonymous with it not happening. They believe that acting young and looking relatively young somehow freezes the aging process. Although this avoidance factor could cause problems, it does keep one focused on the positive. However, it will not eliminate the negative, because the more men hide their feelings, the greater their fears grow. Only those whose fears become so overwhelming and out of control will seek help. The rest will live with this underlying desperation that control is floating away; this is a feeling that will grow rather than diminish in the years to come.

Men will want to find new ways to have control. And as they become aware of this inevitability, new ways of expressing themselves will emerge. Women will say that men are mellowing, but it's just a redirection of the male power source manifesting manhood in other ways to still feel in charge of our lives and the aging process. Realizing this situation exists is a marketer's dream. Do you have products and services that can appeal to these basic ego-centric and emotional needs that can be a bridge from the late 40s into the 50s and beyond?

Men Need Help to Gracefully Grow Older

Levis did it with looser fits for the maturing male's changing body. They didn't ask the consumer to sacrifice style for comfort, so the choice was easy. Hair colorings, transplants, and toupées (that's the old fashioned word, today they're hairpieces or weaves) are popular with men of all ages. However, the guy who is 50+ and worried about that control thing is a hot prospect for anything that keeps a man looking virile and energetic, if not younger—from contact lenses and eyeglass frames, to clothes and even plastic surgery. Fitness and the gear for these activities such as bikes, skates, sports attire, and sportier or faster cars, are all outward feel-good solutions.

And what about the inner man? Healthy eating, vitamins and supplements, diet plans, exercise machines, even Viagra and other prescriptions enhance the quality of life. Then there's the true self, the real man, which is the mind, soul, and spirit. Self help, if not sold in a "touchy feely" way, is a potentially awesome industry. Tony Robbins proved that. But who has what the 50+ males want? Who can address these needs and not cause embarrassment or too much discomfort? Those who do understand the 50+ man have a big market waiting for them. Getting to the little boy inside and bringing out the creative and fun loving part of the 50+ Boomer is both the challenge and opportunity. As this market gets more in touch with its mortality, spiritual considerations provide more viable answers to the growing number of questions this group will have. Helping men get over their innate resistance to change will go a long way in overcoming fear. Marketers who make life easier for Cutting-Edge Boomer males will eventually become a friend with whom they want to do business.

Women Want to Be Appreciated

The concept of women becoming invisible is disturbingly multi-faceted. That's because women perform so many different functions throughout society in general and within individual relationships. During the last century, men have claimed the position of the hub by being the providers while women have assimilated into the role of building the spokes, which support and bring the entire wheel together; therefore, women always had some influence. This influence grew as equality issues gained attention over the years, but it was the Cutting-Edge Boomer women who learned how to harness this power. Because women account for the biggest part of the 50+ population, marketers must acknowledge their importance by catering to their needs and wants, as well as their purchasing decisions.

The Cutting-Edge Boomer woman has been working hard for over 30 years. She has played more roles than a second-level contract player in the old days of Hollywood. All of the household responsibilities, plus going to work every day, has taken its toll both mentally and physically. These women have accomplished so much, and they've literally handled everything thrown their way. Instead of giving women the accolades they richly deserve, society tends to take their superlative actions for granted. Society's lack of recognition certainly treats women over 50 as if they are invisible.

Obstacles, like glass ceilings and other business barriers, were challenged by the Boomer women on behalf of all women. Nonetheless, those who wanted more in the workplace usually got more and they brought a lot of women with them. Struggles in the workplace did not harden the female Cutting-Edge Boomers' hearts. Aside from those on the radical fringe, most look at their job as what they do, not who they are. Women worked to help support their families as well as themselves, and this function was usually a means to an end and not an end in itself. Women were more likely to change the job than have it change them. So women over 50 in the workplace will not be as concerned about a loss of control, as she will be with being prepared for the rest of her life.

Being over 50 is a time in a woman's life when her world is changing in almost every way. With menopause comes a physical and mental change. Their children have left or are about to leave home, and many Cutting-Edge Boomers are becoming first-time grandparents. Husbands are becoming increasingly difficult because of their own control issues, and women who aren't married may feel totally alone. While all this is going on, there's still a future to plan for along with the financial concerns that go with the prospect of probably living many years without a mate.

Through all this, women want to build relationships. They want their family to be happy, and they want the world to be a better, healthier and safer place. They feel that voting can help make a difference and they've made their opinions known at the polls. Although some skeptics gripe that women vote with their hearts rather than with their heads, these critics will just have to listen and understand what's important to the female voter, do something about it, then market that point-of-view in an appealing manner to capture their vote. Because relationships are important to women, a politician or a company better build one with the savvy decision-making 50+ women. You can't reach women in the same old ways with the same old messages. Women are independent and are looking for personal solutions to a variety of problems. They are tough customers even though they have plenty on their mind, so take time to know them before trying to sell to them.

One thing you need to know for sure is that the Cutting-Edge Boomer woman still wants to feel pretty, and she still wants to be noticed. She wants to be treated in a special way, which assures her that she is not invisible. Flattering fashions are important, but not young people's fashions. Creams and lotions, the right hair color and style, contact lenses, wrinkle removal, liposuction (men are doing this too) and anything else that promises to keep her looking younger will be of interest to this consumer. As a marketer, you can provide goods and services to answer problems and fulfill the everyday needs of this growing population. Instill them with hope and give them help—that's the way to win them over.

Many of these women are exploring continued education. They're studying not to get ahead in business but for an intellectual curiosity, or to learn about things that might be helpful in the future. For instance, education in financial matters is big these days; pursuing travel interests or learning more about particular hobbies is fun and fascinating; genealogy has become a way to pass the family's history on to those who follow. The common thread running through these pursuits is that they can all be enjoyed via the Internet or on CD. This makes learning at home so easy and convenient that a big growth spurt in a variety of Internet schooling functions is certain to come from the 50+ women.

Look for self-help to become a burgeoning business once someone like Oprah starts interviewing authors/programmers who have had success in dealing with life over 50. There will be scores of books, CDs, seminars and interactive programs addressing these sensitive areas. The results should be stronger, wiser, more self-assured women, resulting in the women feeling more visible and therefore more in control.

Through the understanding and help of marketers like you, both men and women can gain greater confidence in themselves. Once they become better equipped to deal with their lives now and in the years ahead, they can make a difference to those they come in contact with, like family, friends and society in general.

Chapter 4

What The 50+ Boomers Are Like and what They Want

Understanding the characteristics of the 50+ Boomer is the first step in building a relationship with them and ultimately tying this into the goods and services you offer. When developing a strategy to effectively reach and motivate this powerful buying group, you've got to get into their minds before trying to get into their pocket-books. Here is a list of the important characteristics that will help you know more about this group.

Crucial Characteristics of the 50+ Boomers

Independent

This characteristic is manifested in their thinking and their actions. It is what separates the Cutting-Edge Boomer from other consumers. They are growing more and more independent and influenced less by their peers than younger consumers tend to be. That's why fads are embraced by youth and ignored by the mature consumer. The good news is the latter group will stay with the brands that appeal to them on a personal level rather than those that are chosen because of peer pressure. Creating marketing messages that appeal to their sense of individualism is an effective way to get these mature Boomers to respond.

Adventurous

This is demonstrated by their attitude towards trying new things. This includes traveling to exotic places, exploring the unknown, pushing themselves physically and mentally, tasting new foods, discovering different restaurants, learning new activities and so much more. These 50+ Boomers are a marketer's delight, but not all of them are going to share mutual interests. You've got to talk to and observe Cutting-Edge Boomers until you find the psychographic profile of those that can and will adapt to your product or service, and those that have the potential to be repeat customers. Find out what makes them tick and what their hot buttons are; these are the essential tools needed to help you build a meaningful business.

Open Minded

Here's a trait that was developed early on by these early Boomers. The world had begun to rapidly change as they were in their formative years. More permissive parents and a growing tolerance of others broke down some barriers. Television helped to quickly plant the seeds of change with more impact than was possible in the past. The Vietnam War and the death of President Kennedy bonded this group closer together; thus they became more open to the ideas of their peers. Many had a "live and let live" attitude, which they carry in their lives today on a broader scale. This may apply to how the 50+ Boomer thinks on the social scale, but when it comes to choosing products and services, they take a narrow look at what they're buying because their focus is still about "what's in it for me?"

Giving

At first, this seems to be the antithesis of the "Me" generation. However, there is personal joy in providing help for those less fortunate. Additionally, giving something back to the society in which they live has had a strong influence on many of the 50+

Boomers, and some look at giving as a way to be acknowledged for posterity. Whatever the motive, giving is, and will continue to be, part of this group's legacy. They'll make financial and personal time contributions, or donate cars, clothes and other belongings to causes with which they can identify.

Inclusive

Growing up with the civil rights and feminist movements, and getting a broad view of the perils of segregation and discrimination, helped to mold the accepting attitudes of the early Boomers. This has not changed how individuals within this group live as much as how they perceive the way the world should be. Although there are still plenty of prejudices to overcome, many of the 50+ Boomers tend to believe in equal opportunities for all. They have tried to instill this concept into the belief system of their children, who are practicing today what their parents preached. The Boomers still want to live and associate with people who are more like them than not. However, religion, and to a lesser extent race, have given way to lifestyle similarities in establishing affinity preferences.

Sensitive

Through the guidance of the women in this group, the 50+ Boomers have developed an awareness of their own being and their relationships with others. The 50+ Boomers seem to understand the needs of others and have empathy for community as well as individual problems, yet the men may still resist outwardly showing this characteristic. Social and spiritual solutions are often viewed as different sides of the same coin. As they continue to mature, the Cutting-Edge Boomer will try to bring sanity to the situations confronting them. Therefore, they will apply compassion as well as reason to solve problems.

Realistic

Having lived through a half-century of ups and downs, dreams and disappointments, good days as well as bad, this crowd knows what life is all about. They have learned to expect the unexpected: to plan for the future, yet live for today. Most are optimistic about what life has in store for them. Although there's been a shift to pragmatism, these consumers still want some hope along with help when choosing goods and services.

Value Oriented

The Cutting-Edge Boomer is looking at what they get for the money they spend. The actual cost is relative to how well the product performs, or how good they feel as a result of using the product. Remember: combining quality, service and price equals value. The mature consumers may not always know what they want, but they do know what they don't want. Unless the want aspect is satisfied, you can't expect consumers to select what you offer. Price is the last consideration, not the first.

Caring

With age has come the opportunity to care for others. It may be a spouse, a child or parents that need the care, and tending to the needs of others creates an understanding that people need other people in order to survive. This understanding has softened the "Me" generation. As they become more involved with others and more committed to their well-being, the 50+ Boomers may lead the way to what might be the called the "We" generation. There is a growing interest on trying to make life a little better by doing good things rather than by just talking about good things to do.

Moral Values

This aging segment of the population has passed the "party hardy" period, raised children and is now starting to interact with grandchildren. As they look at how moral values have changed and consider the direction in which these could move, small changes are expected to take place. Fidelity in relationships, respect for elders, even a return to religion are priorities for many 50+ Boomers. Marketers must be aware of these adjustments and be prepared to reflect these new values in the way they communicate with this developing audience.

Experienced

The education of the Cutting-Edge Boomers has been in all facets of their lives. They've learned what works for them, what tastes good, what makes them feel good, what can be depended upon, what constitutes value and how to handle the decision-making process for most categories of goods and services. As a result, the 50+ Boomer is an extremely capable consumer. Because of their super purchasing power, proper appeals to them could deliver favorable purchase decisions for marketers who understand this consumers' particular needs and wants.

Concerned

Through thoughtful reflection, many of the 50+ Boomers have realized that life can only be as good as they allow it to be. They have some trepidation about the future, yet believe that everything will work out. Additionally, they want to make a contribution to their loved ones' and their own well-being. Once these personal concerns have been satisfied, they are prepared to reach out to the extended interests of community and beyond. Helping them overcome personal fears and accomplish their goals of financial security, good health and happiness will go a long way in building a relationship with these consumers.

Vision

This generation has been blessed with the ability to always be looking ahead. From the beginning, society told the Cutting-Edge Boomers that they were special and could attain their dreams. Even when falling short, the 50+ Boomers led the way in education, income, and quality of life. No generation before them has achieved the standard of living that they reached. With such good fortune, they don't appear to be ready to stop now. As they move toward retirement, expect them to be the catalyst for Social Security change—better yet, affordable health care and even education reform for their grandchildren. No one group has done more to build this country to its position of world leadership and they're not finished making an impact.

Now you have an appreciation for the personal characteristics of the 50+ Boomers. They share these in varying degrees with other groups. However, when matched up with the following purchasing considerations, which are key to the Cutting-Edge Boomers, you'll be holding the information necessary to effectively market to this highly desirable audience.

Purchasing Considerations Affecting the Cutting-Edge Boomers

Comfort

The primary desire for the 50+ consumers is to improve the quality of their lives with as much ease and as little hassle as possible. They want to feel good about their decisions and enjoy using what they purchased to enhance their lifestyles. However, circumstances change, such as the kids leaving, health concerns and financial considerations, so many purchasing situations will need to be evaluated by this growing group of consumers. They want the information required to make the right decisions, but will not respond favorably when overwhelmed by too much information, pushy sales people or if scare tactics are used. The better they feel about what they're about to buy, the greater the opportunity is that they will buy.

Financial Impact

As lives change, budgets adjust accordingly. Freedom from earlier financial responsibilities gives way to future financial concerns. Spending for travel and hobbies may have to be weighed against the need to cut back and accommodate a reduced work schedule and saving for retirement. These 50+ Boomers won't be frivolous with their money, however they will continue buying what they want and paying the price for what they believe is the proper product or service to suit their particular needs.

Health/Wellness

Experiencing health problems, or concerns about them in the future, are increasing as the better educated and still somewhat self-obsessed Boomers continue to age. They want to address situations now to keep them looking and feeling better longer. Many have taken precautionary steps with better eating plans and exercise programs along with vitamin supplements in an effort to prolong their youth. And once they've found the combination that works for them, it's not unusual for them to talk about it. So if you have a product or service that improves or supports better health and wellness get to the 50+ Boomer group. If you deliver what you promise, they'll do the word-of-mouth advertising for you.

Enjoyment

"If it feels good, do it." That's an attitude left over from the 60s, but today's Boomer is looking for enjoyment in all aspects of their lives—at home, at work, and in their leisure time. The concept of enjoyment goes beyond fun. It includes satisfaction and achievement, as well as pure pleasure. These consumers want buying experiences to be enjoyable. You won't accomplish this through scare tactics or high-pressure sales pitches. Those who are marketing insurance, home improvement products, security systems, pre-need funeral arrangements and automobiles must remember and embrace the 50+ Boomers' need for enjoyment. Marketers of all other categories must take heed as well.

Convenience

Making it easy for the 50+ Boomer to make a purchase can clinch the sale once they decide this is the product or service for them. Long lines, busy signals, long periods on hold and bad sales or service representatives will kill the deal in short order. Additionally, confusing instructions, lack of follow-up, and out-of-stocks or inconsistent distribution are also fast turn-offs. All of these could lead to the dreaded brand switch. So, if you build your infrastructure and train the people who are responsible for implementing your program properly, chances are you'll make it easier for the Boomers to do business with you and you'll keep them as loyal customers.

Social Implications

The 50+ Boomer is interested in making this a better world. They still have a social conscience, even if trying to save the world has fallen from the top of the list as the Boomers continue to mature. The Cutting-Edge Boomers contribute time and money to causes they believe in. When given a choice, and providing that the product or service delivers on its performance promise, they'll consider one that is environmentally friendly, contributes a portion of the profits to a cause, or helps the community in some way. They have demonstrated, however, that they're not willing to pay much more to support such promotional efforts. They'd rather select the recipient organization and make the contribution themselves. An example is tuna that claimed it didn't harm the dolphins; it did not cost more and quickly became the consumer's choice. In contrast, Scott Paper's 'Helping Hand' line cost just pennies more than comparable brands but consumers didn't relate strongly enough to the charities involved and the brand faded away.

Relationships

The 50+ Boomers seek to develop a sense of bonding with people as well as products. This means that every time they come in contact with your product or service, bonding development and maintenance must be your primary goal. Making a sale without taking the opportunity to build your relationship with the consumer is putting you in jeopardy. This point is particularly crucial for items that aging Boomers are just starting to purchase, from eyeglasses to prescription drugs to financial and insurance services. The after-sale portion of the transaction is what they will remember most and will determine if they will come back to you or go to someone else in the future. Those who are willing to go the extra mile to demonstrate that they want the business, and are prepared to handle the consumer's needs and will do what's needed to keep them happy, are destined to build a loyal following of satisfied customers.

Adaptability

This factor goes a step beyond convenience. It addresses the expressed needs of how easy it is to use, learn about and ultimately operate a particular product. Technology is part of their lives, but they didn't grow up with today's gadgets being second nature to them. Because Cutting-Edge Boomers have the money, getting them to buy will be greatly dependent on how user-friendly the products are, and how well you can communicate that aspect to this somewhat skeptical audience. With a little education and easy-to-use products, the 50+ Boomers can become early adopters, or certainly more receptive to technological advances. For instance, they should be prime prospects for entertainment equipment such as DVDs, TIVO and high definition TV. They'll be the second wave, however, on personal digital assistants (PDAs) and many of the other computer-oriented devices. Nonetheless, don't discount their interest in tech advancements, as well as everyday products and services. Fitting a product into the perceived lifestyle needs of the 50+ Boomers, and making it easy for them to use, will make the task of buying pleasant for the consumer and profitable for you.

Life Experiences

The 50+ Boomer may not have seen it all, but they sure have seen enough. Not only have they become expert consumers, but they have also learned about parenting and are able to give advice to their children on parenting, so they will buy or influence the sale of many items used in this area. Additionally, they have developed capabilities in personal finance, honed their skills for pursuing their favorite hobbies and have formed opinions about politics and how this country should be run. This makes them a force to be reckoned with as legislative measures are considered, which will have effects on our aging Boomers as they approach retirement.

Benefits Factor

As Boomers mature, they moved from rigid, detail oriented, objective decision-making to more flexible, broader, middle-of-the road, subjective evaluations. In a marketing environment this is a move from feature to benefit orientation. It does not mean that the former elements aren't part of the process, rather it's just that these savvy consumers can cut through the other stuff very quickly and get to the real crux of the matter, "what's in it for me?" Emphasizing clear benefits is how you must fashion your communication efforts. Selling to a more seasoned audience requires different purchasing propositions than with a younger audience.

Value

This point is such a major factor it bears repeating. To the 50+ Boomer, low price is not necessarily synonymous with good value. Younger consumers tend to want to get the most for their money. This is a far cry from the concept that quality, service and price equal value. The former group is more peer oriented and therefore will sacrifice some product attributes to be in style; this is part of our disposable society. The Boomers want durability, even though they've grown up in a world of forced obsolescence. That's why you must always provide them with the benefit story of the product, to help make the purchase decision on their terms rather than push your features on them.

Nostalgic Influence

Maybe the good old days weren't all they were cracked up to be, but the Cutting-Edge Boomers have fond memories of them. They still like the Beatles, Elvis and Rock 'n Roll music from their era. They'll tune in to *Nick at Nite*, and some of the movies on AMC are right up their alley. Boomers remember their first date, cruising the boulevard and going shopping or to the ballgame with their friends. They fondly recall getting married and having children. The good times always make for good memories and tend to invoke the innocent humor of days gone by. Reminding those who have just entered the second half of life about the special moments in their lives makes you an instant friend; you become part of the nostalgia that makes the present a little more bearable, a little less hectic and the problems not as pressing. Don't treat the good old days in a patronizing manner or you'll be on the outside looking in. Use it as a way to take down some of the natural defenses these people have toward advertising, and link your product or service with the message in a way that lets this audience know you understand them.

Security/Peace of Mind

If comfort is the roof of the house under which all these buying triggers reside, then security and peace of mind are shoring the foundation of the structure. The security of financial well-being due to a good job, a place to live and independence in the future are important building blocks. Hope for continued good health, for themselves and their loved ones, adds strength to the foundation. And freedom from worry about personal safety forms the base on which their very existence is built. Without these securities and the peace of mind that comes with them, there would be little confidence in the future; therefore, there would be no incentive to consume other than to provide for the most basic of needs. Is your marketing effort appreciative of the importance of security and peace of mind?

There you have it: the characteristics, which make up the mindset of the 50+ Boomers coupled with the purchasing considerations that mold their actions. Naturally, your own qualitative and quantitative research will produce a list that is unique to your specific products or services. Nonetheless, this list of characteristics and purchasing considerations is a good place to start. Add your understanding and experience to it and you'll be well on the way to developing a meaningful marketing program aimed at the 50+ Boomer.

Chapter 5

THE 50+ BOOMERS ARE LEADING A GENERATION OF INDIVIDUALS

As you re-evaluate the marketing efforts being applied to Cutting-Edge Boomers, be aware that this is not a homogenous cluster of consumers all wanting the same things and ready to respond to the same stimuli. Yes, there are similarities just as there are vast differences within this group.

There will be differences because these mature consumers have become more individualistic. They think for themselves and are interested in self-expression. Personalized and customized products and services help to fill their perceived needs. Have you ever listened to a group of Cutting-Edge Boomers order dinner? "Hold this, light on that, something on the side, can I substitute what he's having for what I was supposed to get?" But they all come back together by sharing "One dessert, with extra forks please." The 50+ Boomers have learned to ask for what they want, yet they stay within their acceptable boundaries. Marketers need to understand this form of expression and act accordingly.

It's All About Choice

The Henry Ford approach of offering the customer "any color car they want, as long as it's black" won't work with Cutting-Edge Boomers. They like the concept of "have it your way," but the smart marketer will take it one step further. Give the consumer the option of building it their way from scratch. This can deliver additional sales and satisfied customers at the same time. The pizza people have done it for years by encouraging the patron to add on the toppings of choice and charging extra for each one.

Buying a Car Is Not Fun

Don't get greedy like the car manufacturers, and have all the amenities and extras already included so that there are no choices. Consumers can now get the colors they want, but have little say about the options; that's not very smart marketing. To begin with, the basic model of a car could be advertised at a lower starting price. I don't mean promoting one without wheel covers, air conditioning or even floor mats, but all the other extras could be upsell opportunities. When presented properly, Cutting-Edge Boomers could understand the value of having the night vision package, a version of a global positioning system (GPS) for emergencies and even heated seats. The way it is offered now is if it's on the car you get it, otherwise, pick another car. It becomes a matter of settling for a vehicle with more than what you want or less than you want; it's never just what you want.

I'm sure that the auto-sales people will disagree, but perhaps they haven't bought a car lately. Every three years it's time for me to lease a new car. The process is the same as buying; the terms are just different. The last four cars were the same make and model, and not much about the car has changed, so color has been the primary difference. However, the option packages have been different each time. Adding some things and eliminating others was not an option. The add-ons would have exceeded the take-aways, but the infrastructure of automobile marketing doesn't allow for this kind of individualization, customization or personalization.

Going Out in Style

It's funny, the auto industry won't give you what you want but the funeral people will. There's a whole new trend called "memorialization." That's an industry term for "individualization," "customization" and "personalization." Instead of traditional somber services and standard resting places, people are choosing to actually celebrate the life of a loved one or their own. Cremation is increasing in popularity and so are the options: scattering, shooting ashes into space, urns depicting lifestyles, glass-fronted niches for the remains with a photo and memorabilia are all part of this movement. The services have taken on a new flavor as well. Jazz, Country Western, or whatever kind of music was preferred, will send off the deceased. Many people are making their decisions for themselves and not letting others do it for them. People want to determine how they're going to be remembered and the manner in which their death is to be handled. And guess who's putting the "Me" in memorialization? You got it—the 50+ Boomers. Many are helping their parents make final arrangements, and while they're doing it these sons and daughters are consciously, or subconsciously, making pre-need plans for themselves.

This is revolutionizing the deathcare industry. New products and services are required to support personalization—everything from video obituaries, to custom-painted caskets and urns to party planners for the celebration. The high cost of dying won't matter to those who want to make a statement. If they're willing to spend $30,000 for a car, which they'll drive for just a few years, how much are they willing to pay for a service and a permanent memorial designed to last for generations? The Boomers have always wanted to make their mark in life, now they can carry this desire to the next step. Making per-need arrangements not only allows people to express their wishes, but it also has the added benefit of easing the burden for those left behind.

Choosing Your Cruising

Cruise lines have realized that choices are important to the 50+ consumer. As an example, not long ago there was one dining room on a ship and two sittings for meals. Today, the consumer is being encouraged to set their own time for eating, select from a number of on-board restaurants and to choose whether to dress formally or casually. More options are also being offered for on-board activities as well as on-shore excursions. Princess Cruises calls it *Personal Choice Cruising*. Of course the traditional arrangements are still available for those who prefer them. You can bet the Cutting-Edge Boomer was the potential cruise audience that prompted this change. This is an appropriate progression in making cruising a more enjoyable and personal experience for even the seasoned traveler. Firms that emphasize the grueling activities and adventure really missed the boat on what truly appeals to the target audience of 50+ Boomers. Studying what the cruise business is doing to accommodate individual wants could be helpful in determining what might improve your particular business with these consumers.

Packaged Goods Can Provide Service Too

Grocery store products also have the opportunity to provide individualization. Brands will have difficulty doing it from a product standpoint, but they do have many service options. Multi-category brands such as Healthy Choice, are notable exceptions. They can provide brand synergy across a wide range of products, but they still require personalized service as a means to customize for the 50+ Boomers. Meal planning and recipe suggestions are the obvious starting points. The Internet is the ideal vehicle to help packaged-goods marketers get a relationship started. A website recognizing the different needs of the various audiences and one that accepts questions, and allows for email dialogue, will go a long way in meeting the personal needs of Cutting-Edge Boomers. Tens of thousands of brands fight for survival on the supermarket shelves, so building a relationship with specific segments like the 50+ Boomers can yield profitable results.

Forget 'One Size Fits All'

Just as it's not sound marketing to lump maturing Boomers into one group, it's not feasible to tailor products, services and advertising into individual elements. However, it is possible and very wise to segment this audience as you would any other broad group. Then it becomes a matter of matching what you're offering with the various segments, identifying the costs required to capture a share of the market and determining if that market provides long-term profit potential. This is something you would do when considering any new or expanded market opportunities, so why not give this group the same scrutiny and ultimately the same respect.

Not all Cutting-Edge Boomers are married, nor are they all Empty-Nesters or all upper income, the same religion, race or nationality, the list of differences goes on and on. Remember, you used to target these people when they were a younger more desirable audience. The demographics haven't changed that much. Most of those who claimed religious beliefs back then still do. Those who were doing well financially still have money and those who didn't have money are still struggling.

Extrapolating from the U.S. Census (1998), you will discover that about 80 percent of the 50+ Boomers are white, 10 percent black, and 8 percent Hispanic, with Asian around 3 percent. The racial demographic of the youngest 5-year group of Boomers will be about 73 percent white, 12 percent black, over 10 percent Hispanic, and just under 4 percent Asian. So some change is on the way but not enough to alter the basic ethnic composition of the Cutting-Edge from the Trailing Boomers.

There are many other opportunities to individualize, customize, and personalize products and services. Insurance firms can bring together whole life policies with long-term care and annuities packaged in programs designed to shift coverage in one area while funding it from another, depending on people's particular circumstances. It's not too early to discuss these options with the 50+ Boomer and to help them make the right decisions.

The publishing industry could learn about what the 50+ consumer needs now and will probably need in the future. The fact that those over 50 spend about twice as much annually on books (U.S Bureau of Labor Statistics, Consumer Expenditure Survey, 1996) than younger consumers makes Cutting-Edge Boomers an important target. Self-help books directed at this audience are an obvious category, and one that is sure to expand. These books will have to be segmented to suit the various groups (e.g. spirituality will deal with different religions, believers and not, those who practice and those who don't, and so forth). How-to books, from hobbies to finances to caregiving, are also going to be in demand, but they should be targeted to the 50+ Boomer, not just the general market. Even fiction will need to consider the age of heroes and heroines and how they relate to Cutting-Edge Boomers.

You can analyze the numbers provided by various research studies or read through endless pages of the Statistical Abstract and still not know much about the 50+ Boomer. You'll have a better appreciation of the size and scope of the market, but what is this person or this group of people really like? This is where feelings become more important than facts. So whenever you are presented with demographic information, be sure to consider the psychographic or lifestyle ramifications of the data.

Chapter 6

HOW TO SAVE YOUR RELATIONSHIP WITH THE 50+ BOOMER

The absolute worst thing a marketer can do is take consumers for granted; it's the kiss of death. Yet many seemingly smart and savvy advertisers are doing just that when it comes to the 50+ Boomers.

Maybe it is like a marriage of thirty or more years where the romance is gone but the couple stays together. Too much time has passed and too little effort has been put into keeping the interest level up. As a result, the flame has died or at least subsided, but to paraphrase an old song, "if there's still a spark, the flame can burn again." There is hope if both parties accept that there really is a problem with the relationship and want to do something about it. The road back may require some soul searching, therapy, remedial action and careful, ongoing monitoring in order to get things back on track. The same efforts are necessary when a marketing relationship gets stagnant or turns sour, with the problem resting squarely on the shoulders of the marketer.

The truth is that many marketers do not even realize that they have a relationship problem. It is not because awareness has fallen off; rather it is an attitude thing. In other words, the consumer still knows about you, but they somehow have the notion that you do not care about them. This is a difficult nuance for many marketers to comprehend. Let's say, for example, that you have improved your product or service. The feature list is longer and the benefits more impressive and what you offer is a terrific value. So you should have a competitive advantage. Then, why haven't you been able to garner a greater share of market? Could it be the relationship factor?

Put Your Money into the Right Markets

With a thorough review of the marketing strategy and an honest evaluation of the tactical implementation of the program, you'll discover some important people are not being targeted effectively. Check out what your message is and the manner in which it's delivered. Check out the media mix and evaluate the audience your radio and TV schedule is reaching, or review the profile of the readers exposed to the print campaign. Then compare how much of your advertising dollars are being invested into the various age segments. If you're like many marketers, the bulk of the spending was for the 18 to 49 or the 25 to 49 age groups.

How much is allocated to those 50 to 54 and those 55+? Don't fudge. What I want to do is challenge you to open your eyes, and start thinking of new ways to build your business by capturing a market that you can reach out and gather in without turning your entire marketing effort upside down. Unless you have a product or service that is considered an older skew—such as denture adhesive, "safe" investments, cruises with a two-week duration, or cemetery property—the possibilities of your plan overlooking the 50+ market is surprisingly high.

Let's say that you are not ignoring the 50+ market from a media standpoint. Conventional wisdom suggests that a number of people who are younger, like 45 year olds, listen to, watch or read the same media as those who are older than 50. The problem may not be *whom* you are reaching, it could be the message you're presenting and *how* you're delivering it.

Do older Boomers respond to the same stimuli as 25 year olds? That's an obvious question with an obvious answer, "No." Equally as dangerous is talking to these Boomers as if they are old. People 55+ believe they look at least 5 years younger than their age and feel 10 years younger. So you must be careful, and not talk to them as if they are children. And certainly don't treat them like their parents.

If the media is not reaching them, or the message is not relating to them, what else might be missing? Take a look at the rest of the marketing mix: the product, the package, the pricing, and the promotion, even the distribution profile if applicable. All of these elements can contribute to how well you do with Cutting-Edge Boomers.

Don't Throw the Boomers Out with the Eight-Tracks

The product you currently offer may have become a commodity, yet still has relevance to an aging audience. LaSueur Peas sold by Green Giant are a viable brand to most 50+ Boomers but have no significance to the young crowd. One group will pay more and the other group could care less. Another consideration is that what's obsolete to some may not yet be to others. No, I am not suggesting that there is a rebounding market for eight-track tapes, but not all mature consumers are willing to drop old favorites too quickly. Just because a product has matured, it doesn't mean it has reached the end of its life cycle.

By the same token, some people waste their time lowering the usage age of a product while ignoring the heavy user or actually turning them off. For example, a TV commercial for a cruise line, backed up by a high-intensity music track, showed people rock climbing, rollerblading on deck, jet skiing and wind surfing, as what to expect when you book passage on their line. Obviously, they chose the right networks to air the spots because I was exposed to these images with some frequency. However, based on my experience, the ad was completely off target. I have cruised for years, and I've observed that most age groups enjoy the variety of activities currently offered. I like the peace and quiet of having coffee on deck at sunrise, the walk or jog around the promenade, relaxing, reading, eating, being entertained and maybe participating in some group activities. In port, the days are busy sightseeing and shopping. That's what people do who cruise. I wonder if the campaign brought in enough younger, first-time cruisers to offset the established audience they pushed away.

Another warning, be careful about using a "has been," or "never was" older celebrity to pitch your product or service. Chances are that unless they are instantly recognizable and in some way relevant to the product and service being offered, the celebrity can get in the way. People aren't motivated to buy because of the spokesperson's age; they buy because the product or service is perceived to deliver something they want. The operative word, of course, is "want." They may need it, but if they do not want it you will not make the sale. The right spokesperson can help; the wrong one can get in the way or even lose the sale if they aren't able to enhance the product relationship with the consumer.

Proper Packaging Can Be a Plus

Even with the right product, you can still miss the 50+ Boomer audience if your packaging is not right for them. Packaging can take several forms and applies to both products and services. I am not just referring to package graphics, although that's a good place to start. If it's an impulse purchase, the design can make or break you at the point-of-purchase (POP). Most marketers want a package that presents the brand name and personality, along with the key product promise, to as broad an audience as possible.

Packaging can actually turn off consumers before they consider what is inside. As the Boomers move on in age, the package will become an increasing part of the purchasing decision. What's your package like, whom does it appeal to, what message does it send, and whom might it deter from buying?

At least with the Cutting-Edge Boomers, bigger isn't necessarily better. For years, the trend has been to move up in size. Get the consumer to buy more and they will use your product longer before repurchasing, thereby making it their current brand. Also, because so much of the cost goes into the package itself, the consumer can realize a savings, while at the same time, the manufacturer does not have to take a shorter margin. By adding sizes, marketers can secure more shelf space and create a stronger brand billboard in their section of the store. This practice has subsided since slotting allowances make it too expensive to add sizes indiscriminately. Category managers at the chain-buying level keep a careful eye on how well every size performs for each brand.

Now the consideration may be for you to add smaller sizes to accommodate the Empty-Nesters or single-person household. That might add to the packaging costs, but it could fill a need in a growing niche. Multi-packs could bring the costs per transaction down and provide enough product to keep the customer out of the marketplace longer. As for shelf space, maybe it is time to get rid of your least popular, probably least profitable size, and replace it with a size that's friendly to the 50+ consumer. And, while you're at it, take a look at the typeface and type size. Is it easy to read and large enough for aging eyes? A number of older shoppers don't like to use reading glasses as they move about the store, so they avoid products whose labels aren't buyer friendly.

In service businesses, packaging takes on a slightly different and more subtle meaning, but it is quantifiable nonetheless. Bring all of the elements of your advertising, including website promotion, public relations and collateral materials together in a cohesive and related manner. In other words, these activities should be tied up in a tidy little package. When properly done, the synergy factor applies and a strong image emerges. If the execution is piece-meal, the result can be a complete mess.

Graphics as well as tone dictate who embraces your brand personality and who rejects it. Should you use illustrations, computer-generated graphics or photographs to present your pictorial story? This determines what your service package looks like and positions your brand with consumers, but that means it probably will not appeal to all consumers. If you want to attract the 50+ Boomer, are you appealing to them or turning them away?

For instance, while computer graphics may appeal to a younger crowd, they are not broadly accepted or understood by an older audience. Photographs using people can bring warmth and humanity to your service image, but be careful not to show only one age group or a single ethnicity unless they're all you want as customers. Illustrations straddle the fence between the two worlds and may be a safe compromise.

Experienced Consumers Are the Most Loyal Consumers

Experience in making buying decisions is a big bonus with the 50+ consumer. The 50+ Boomers have years of use in the categories they've been purchasing, and these consumers know what works for them and why. That's where loyalty works for the incumbent brands. But if there are changes in the consumer's needs or the competitor has improved the products, or the competitor's positioning is perceived as better meeting this consumer's needs, the possibility of a brand switch comes into the marketing equation.

Price only comes into the decision-making process when the educated consumer is resisting what is being offered or a side-by-side comparison is made. The 50+ consumer has years of experience in buying goods and services, and is used to paying for what they think they need. Virtually everything is bought because it fills an emotional need, but that decision is backed up with a rationale, be it real or imagined. For virtually every purchase, the consumer has evaluated the decision on the criterion that "quality plus service plus price equals value." Give them the quality and service level they're looking for and the price can be justified nine times out of ten. The degree to which the consumer goes through this process takes just a matter of seconds when shopping for groceries, as an example. It takes longer when it is a considered purchase like a car, and somewhere in between for durable goods or mid-range services. In any event, the Boomer's decision will be greatly influenced by their impression of your company or brand, and as a result of the packaging and advertising. If you have not established value, price is simply an excuse not to buy.

I am not suggesting that you can sell commodities for twice the price of the competition if there really is no perceivable difference. In that case, the moment of truth will be at the point of purchase. However, if the consumer believes you have something worth more, they will pay more for it. Your own ongoing research and the competitive atmosphere in the marketplace will best determine how high this price threshold is.

Old Products for a New Market and New Products for an Older Market

A new buying situation in which older Boomers are finding themselves in is purchasing products and services they have not needed to use in the past: arthritis medications, a home computer, or a car instead of a mini-van. Do not lump them in with their parents when it comes to over-the-counter (OTC) medicines. If you are marketing technology, do not treat them like kids who are looking at electronic gear for probably very different applications. Do not treat them like kids who are looking at electronic gear in a different way for probably very different applications. Be sure to approach these mature adults with respectful understanding, and don't dwell on the fear factor when educating them about the advantages of preparing for the future by purchasing the proper insurance protection now.

For services, new purchases may involve the full-range of financial offerings from bonds and mutual funds, to retirement insurance. Travel, without the kids, opens up a whole world of possibilities. And of course, pre-arrangements for funeral and burial services start to become viable considerations after one turns 50.

Unless you have truly deep pockets, not just to outspend the competition in your category, but to breakthrough the clutter of all advertising, your marketing message must get the attention of your audience the first time they're exposed to it. Next, you must grab their interest and create an instant desire to have what you are offering. The clincher is then to cause the consumer to take the appropriate actions, which will result in a sale. Why are these steps so important with the Boomer audience? It's because they have been exposed to so much advertising and promotion for so many years, they have become jaded, if not numb, to most advertising. Some of their old ways of thinking have to be altered to allow new concepts to get through and become established in the brains of the 50+ consumers.

The attitude of many Boomers is, "If I'm happy with what I'm using in a given category, why even consider a change." Fads won't move them, so it takes a real understanding of what makes them tick in order to garner a primary sell or cause a brand switch. We will discuss this crucial area, along with how to use media more effectively, a little later.

Now let's get back to the elements of the marketing mix. Promotion and distribution have yet to be addressed. These two areas encompass a wide range of possibilities and deserve careful consideration. From cents-off coupons to temporary price reductions, loyalty discounts to sweepstakes enticements, the Boomers have seen it all. Yet there are some promotional approaches that seem to fare better than others. For example, it is difficult to reach young consumers through traditional print media, but it is a viable consideration for Cutting-Edge Boomers, particularly as they age. Before creating coupon ads and adding a bunch of newspapers and those food and shelter publications to the media schedule, factor in the 50+ Boomers' lifestyle.

The Boomers Are Not Sitting Ducks

Most people 55 and under are quite busy. Cutting-Edge Boomer women have been, and still are, working women. They worked to help buy a house, to send the kids to college, to pay for vacations and to improve the quality of life for themselves and their families. Many have outperformed their husbands in the workplace. Still others have worked just to make ends meet or to house and feed the children. In all instances, the one thing these women have in common is a lack of time. Raising a family, keeping house and working makes virtually every moment precious to this generation of "wonder women." Few of them have time to spend with their daily newspapers and even fewer look to the homemaker magazines for help. They do have an inclination to go through the Saturday and Sunday papers, so free standing inserts (FSI) work for food and related products, as do retailer inserts and certain sections of the weekend newspapers. For the man of the house, those who get a paper browse through it mostly every day. Sports and Business are particularly good sections for advertising sales and promotions.

For men and women, magazines directed to their business and personal interests are good places for general and promotional ads. Direct Mail, although it is expensive on an individual basis, can deliver a more personalized message to either men or women. To reach the upscale woman Boomer, take a look at the city magazines and the local versions of the theater publications. These deliver an amazingly responsive audience and ads or promotions can be changed monthly. These magazines can do a good job of reaching men as well.

TV is still a powerful medium, but there is a very narrow window of time when you can reach these working Boomers. That's prime time, and it's expensive if you buy the broadcast networks. Prime cable can be an option, but the number of viewers on a local basis is often small. Morning news shows and weekend schedules can reach working consumers, but these programs are less targeted toward Cutting-Edge Boomers. Remember, the top rated shows with those under 49 are rarely the top-rated shows with those 50 and older, so choose carefully

Out-of-home media makes sense for the busy Boomer. Of course outdoor media reaches virtually all consumers. On the other hand, radio has become an out-of-home medium as well. The average worker spends over an hour in their car each day. Radio formats can provide narrower targeting, so it's a great medium for reaching Boomers, although you may not reach men and women with the same station mix. Radio gives your message flexibility and production costs are far less than for TV. Plus it's an engaging and imaginative medium that works for branding as well as promotional messages.

What about specific promotions at the retail or sales level? Again, the Boomers know how to buy. They tend to use coupons for new products if they already intended to purchase the product. Most use coupons for brands they know which are on their selection list, and the same thinking applies to temporary price reductions. You must already be approved in the mature consumer's mind before promotional considerations come into play.

Being pre-approved by the consumer comes from years of developing patterns that become buying habits. These are not easily broken. That's why grocers offer club cards with special benefits for cardholders. Other retailers give those using store charge cards extra discounts. And still others have frequent shoppers cards, which get stamped every time one shops there, and freebies or discounts are offered after so many visits. Boomers have been using these loyalty programs for years. They will continue to frequent the same stores, unless given a compelling reason to change.

However, as needs change, shopping patterns change as well. For instance, Empty-Nesters are less likely to shop at club stores or food warehouses than their younger counterparts. The reasons are obvious: They don't need multi-packs of extra-large sizes. They want to have a choice of brands and they don't want to box their own groceries or be subjected to the overwhelming noise or crowds associated with these outlets. So traditional grocers should make a concerted effort to latch on to these consumers. They might even be able to lead them away from the supermarket they've shopped at for years if they provide the sizes and selections these Boomers want. This also applies to specific services they need, such as on-premise butchers who will cut their meat to order. Although two people do not consume as much as a family of four or more, this family of two will be buying their full orders from the same supermarket every week. Those who are buying thirty rolls of paper towels, four cases of soda and enough meat to last a month are probably not buying these items at the supermarket anyway. So which family is really worth more to the store? From a marketer's standpoint, however, you want to be sure you have distribution of the right products in both types of stores.

Another reason for Boomers to change stores is if they change addresses. We are still a mobile society and consumers move on the average of once every five years or so. A big move can occur once the children leave. At that time or shortly there-after, many Empty-Nesters scale down on the size of the house and scale back on mortgage or rent payments. This gives them more disposable income and the confidence to spend it. The move means establishing a whole new collection of stores at which to shop. So get to these older Boomers as soon as they move, become their friend, help them to get comfortable in their new neighborhood and be part of the shopping experience for years to come. Smart marketers will tie in with these retailers to help make it an everybody-wins situation.

There are plenty of opportunities to solidify your product or service as the brand of choice with the 50+ Boomers. Similar opportunities exist to affect a brand switch. It is up to you to determine which factors will sway these savvy consumers to your particular attributes. What you say, how you say it and where you say it will be the ultimate test of how well you really know what motivates the Cutting-Edge Boomers.

Chapter 7

The 50+ Boomer Should Be Considered Before Making Any Marketing Decisions

Prejudice has been described as contempt prior to investigation. I submit that this is the way too many marketers approach the Cutting-Edge Boomers. This point is important enough to revisit over and over until this crest of the Boomer wave receives the attention it deserves. The prejudicial aspect of my contention is not some kind of new civil rights issue; rather it's a matter of dollars and cents. If you're against developing specific strategies and inventive implementations to capture a significant share of this emerging market, the competitor who does recognize their importance is going to eat your lunch!

So let's investigate what the more than 21 million Cutting-Edge Boomer market has to offer you in immediate opportunities, plus what influence they will have on the 20 million consumers directly preceding them and the 55 million Boomers who will follow. According to the U.S. Bureau of the Census (2000), while accounting for only 7% of the population the 50+ Boomers account for 20% of the discretionary income and control 45% of the U.S. financial assets. That explains why 70% of the 50+ Boomers own their own homes, own more luxury vehicles, travel more and in general spend like they have money—because they do have the money.

These financial facts certainly indicate how vital of a consumer the Cutting-Edge Boomer has become. As the next group of Boomers lay claim to the first five years of their 50s, they will generate equally impressive numbers. The rest of the Boomers, whose population is even larger, can be expected to make meaningful gains as well, as they travel through the years. With this kind of purchasing power and the ongoing desire to keep spending, the group can't be ignored, slighted or in anyway overlooked.

Cutting-Edge Boomers are experiencing their peak earning years, so they can spend and save at the same time. And remember, once the children have gone, they'll have an additional $5,000 to $10,000 in annual disposable incomes. That means marketing potential for almost all products and services. Some exceptions would be compact cars, amusement parks (this will change when the grandchildren come of age), term life insurance, risky stocks, three-story condos, most fast foods (again grandchildren will make a difference), reality TV and just about everything tuned to people 20 years younger than they are.

Twenty Years Later

There are three events that came to our attention in 1981 that had little impact on Cutting-Edge Boomers at that time. However, since these events celebrated 20th anniversaries in 2001, taking a closer look at their influence on the 50+ Boomer can provide valuable insight into what's happened and what the marketing landscape looks like now. These are not case histories, just observations about three different occurrences that have become more closely linked over a couple of decades. How you view these thoughts may suggest your predisposed attitudes regarding the 50+ consumer.

The events are: (1) the introduction of the personal computer (PC), (2) Music Television (MTV), and (3) *Headline News* (CNN's sound bite, half-hour report). How did these various launches affect the Cutting-Edge Boomers over the past 20 years and what will they mean in the future? What lessons can be learned by examining the impact each has made from a marketing standpoint?

In 1981, the Cutting-Edge Boomers were all in their 30s. Many of them did not jump into the high-tech world of PCs with both feet. As the need to be computer literate developed in the workplace, more and more Cutting-Edge Boomers responded. However, this group was already busy achieving, so they weren't in the wave of early adopters. Status was a consideration, but necessity was the mother of invention for them becoming PC savvy. Now they've made the PC a part of their lives, although most are not a slave to it. The 50+ Boomer has made the computer and Internet access into a convenient tool to help them accomplish some of what their busy lives demand. The PC will continue to be an important part of the 50+ Boomers' repertoire as they travel on through the second half of life. Yet marketers of PCs and accessories haven't really targeted this affluent audience in ways designed to maximize their business with these consumers. Marketers should be targeting the Boomers for online buying, pushing the digital photography angle for the ever-growing number of grandparents or getting them involved with learning more about products and services through an ongoing Internet marketing effort.

MTV never really targeted Cutting-Edge Boomers; they were past 30 and therefore too old. Today the average age of the MTV viewer is 20. Yet MTV has had a profound effect on the 50+

Boomer. It became a major influence on the children of the Boomers. Many Boomer parents, who were brought up with TV themselves, didn't find it necessary to monitor or enforce rules when it came to their kids watching a bunch of music videos. What harm could there be? Of course, if you're familiar with MTV, you know things have changed over the past 20 years. The music evolved, the format changed, the fashion changed, basically the whole attitude changed. Programming has become bolder with sexy dance moves dominating the screen and sound-bite comedy rounding out the flashy attitude. These changes have been made to appeal to the younger generation's "give it to me fast" attitude. Most Cutting-Edge Boomers are oblivious to what their children have been watching and what effect such programming has had on them.

The children of the 60s were letting the kids of the 80s do their own thing. Many critics claim that this has resulted in a further moral deterioration in our country, but I predict that the Cutting-Edge Boomers are going to be the ones that fix it. Grandparents will hope that their grandchildren will grow up with some of the values learned from their own grandparents. They're going to revisit values with their grandchildren, and as Boomers teach their grandkids, they will relearn these old lessons as well. Family traditions and values all will be part of the Boomer's lives again. This won't make the 50+ Boomers MTV viewers; however, they may have an effect on the quality of the network's programming in an indirect way.

A Change for the Better?

The third part of the trilogy is *Headline News*. When CNN started, the network hoped to get younger, busier viewers, such as the 30-something Cutting-Edge Boomers. They had some luck, but for some time their numbers had been falling off. So the network, formerly headed by "older guy" Ted Turner, is now owned by AOL Time Warner. AOL knows about the Internet, being the number one service provider. Time Warner understands the sound bite mentality of TV news viewers, particularly the younger ones. What do you do with this knowledge? It's simple: format the screen like a website. That's what they appeared to achieve when the new format was unveiled in the late summer of 2001.

I'll describe it in case you haven't seen a *Headline News* broadcast. The top two-thirds of the screen has a talking head (a reporter) taking up most of the screen and a bold block of copy telling you about what they're talking about takes up the rest of the top portion. Below that is a couple lines of superimposed copy relating to another late breaking story. Weather, stock prices or sports scores take up the remaining bottom section, including graphics that change colors as maps of the various sections of the country dissolve in and out.

Maybe my concerns were self-centered, but I didn't like the format the first time. I tuned in a number of other times during the first few months and gave up. TV executives are willing to go to any length to get and keep younger viewers, but they have no reservations about driving older ones away. I learned about the format change by reading the newspaper and wanted to see what was going on. If the only way people knew of the change was through the papers, or if they already were a *Headline News* viewer, then only an older audience tuned in. If they're at all like I am, they've already tuned out. How and when are they going to attract a younger viewer, and if they make adjustments how many of those who were turned off will be agreeable to trying *Headline News* again?

So I spoke to a number of people between the ages 25 and 35. First of all, most of them weren't aware of the new format because they don't watch *Headline News.* When they did watch, they did not have the same problem with the busy screen that I had. In fact, many volunteered that this was more like a combination of a web page with streaming video combined with a regular news broadcast. A few believed that this was the beginning of a move toward interactive TV news, which will certainly become a reality. So we could either be watching history in the making or this concept is too far ahead of the curve.

I'm sure the network executives already know, or will soon determine, what works for the younger audience they are attempting to reach. However, the change seems to be an example of throwing away older consumers before it's even known if the product has a chance of succeeding with a younger group. It's the quantity versus the quality game—agencies and their clients are convinced that younger is better.

Reviewing your options may suggest that concentrating on a younger audience isn't necessarily the answer. It's getting tougher and tougher to reach a younger consumer. There are more media possibilities, including the Internet, to interest them. Your message has to be short and sweet, virtually devoid of information and the ad or commercial must pretend not to be selling. Fads change and any loyalty you've developed can go with it. So why should you put all of your money into the younger consumer, if there's a neglected consumer who likes to spend and is potentially loyal? That's what Madison Avenue seems to be doing, and that's what *Headline News* did. Is that what you're going to do? Get over the prejudice, forget the contempt, have the courage to investigate. There's a whole new consumer waiting for you in the form of the 50+ Boomer.

Chapter 8

Learn from the Masters of Advertising

The Boomers were the first to be raised with television as their friend, their babysitter, and their mentor. TV is a passive medium; all the parents had to do was put the child in front of the tube, turn it on and the programming did the rest. Through the magic of sight and sound the child was easily mesmerized into inactivity, while at least part of the brain remained open to the power of suggestion. So children stayed out of trouble while mom did other things around the house. The medium was also a fantastic learning tool. Network executives discovered early on that TV was a great teacher, and advertisers saw it as a great sales tool. Many of these children learned the words to a jingle from a commercial before they learned their ABCs.

Because the screen does much of the work for the brain, the viewer could pay less attention and still have a sense of what was going on. Reading required concentration, and the radio often called for listener involvement, or at least imagination. More facts could be conveyed through the written or spoken word, but TV related messages with feeling.

Back when the Cutting-Edge Boomers were young, TV gave us instant access to news events, from breaking the barrier of space, to the assassination of a president and to battlefields around the world. These events did not depend on someone else's explanation or interpretation to be meaningful news; we saw it happening before our eyes and often in real time. TV became the popular source for news, but lengthy, in-depth news could not hold people's interest so sound bites became the way of presenting the stories. Sound bites gave the information fast and slick and let the pictures carry the emotion, and those who wanted to be further informed had to go elsewhere. Years later, MTV perfected the sound bite for entertainment purposes. Broadcast news seems to have been reduced down to the shortest possible time spent on any given subject. The sound bite approach has resulted in more information with less content being disseminated to the audience.

Many of the 50+ Boomers are better educated, better informed and better equipped to make decisions than previous generations. However, they don't necessarily delve into things before making their move. Nonetheless, they want to know that facts are available to back up the feelings they have. As they've grown older, however, they have more media to consider for their informational input.

Years of being exposed to thousands of messages each day has caused the Boomers to automatically filter out what they don't think they need and put the decision-making process on a fast forward mode. The successful marketer must carefully craft a way of quickly building a relationship with these consumers, create a need for the product or service and close the sale without any wasted effort. This must be done before the consumer moves on to contemplate another subject.

Both the Medium and the Message Are Important

Few will argue that TV is the 50+ Boomers' medium of choice. However there's a lot of disagreement over how to use this medium most effectively and very little consideration given to what motivates these consumers. There are thousands of ad agencies throughout the country and untold numbers of directors, producers, and writers, and all are involved in creating, producing and bringing commercials into the homes of potential consumers. Unfortunately, many of these people have no idea of what's really on the minds of the viewers, and have no intention of creating a spot that even remotely smacks of selling something. Agency account management and principals, as well as client marketing executives and CEOs, appear to be afraid to insist that advertising's role—yes, it's very existence—is to sell.

Advertising techniques have improved over the years. Production capabilities should get some of the credit, because each time a new medium appeared on the scene, aggressive agency people found ways to better utilize and enhance these new communication vehicles. In the early days, newspapers spawned magazines, and then color became available. Later, space-age technology improved TV broadcasting and led the way to the World Wide Web. Along the way, we took the technical tools out of the hands of professionals and gave them to virtually anyone who operates a computer causing the entire production process to speed up.

At first, the technical advances would appear to be a good thing. In the early days of my career, a four-color print ad took weeks to produce. There was photography or illustration, retouching, plates and proofing before the client saw the work. Later, with the advent of film and chromalins, the time frame was reduced to a few days. Now, with digital photography, computer illustrations and electronic mechanicals, agencies are expected to turn ads around in a matter of hours. The same is true for TV commercials. We used to shoot, see the rushes or dailies, edit on Moviolas, send out for dissolves, view the slop print, add the soundtrack, then make tweaks. We advanced to shooting on film, editing on tape, and collapsing the timeframe to days rather than weeks. Today, shooting digitally and having the on-location computer linked up with the agency and even the client, decisions can be made and changes implemented in real time. Is the result better? Will it sell more products or services?

Unfortunately, new technology and hands-on decision making have caused execution to become more important than the idea. Tactics come before strategies, that is if strategies are even part of the equation. So where does the consumer fall into all of this? Through the cracks is my contention.

Later, I'll talk about how understanding the Boomers, then developing advertising to meet their needs and wants, can help get your creative process back on track. First, let's take a moment to look at what some of the masters of advertising did to advance the art and science of this profession in the formative days of TV.

The Hard Sell

Rosser Reeves, the father of hard sell, believed in driving home a product's point-of-differentiation. He believed in discovering or inventing the single selling point which, when effectively demonstrated and backed by heavy media frequency, would convince consumers that a particular brand was superior to all others, thus making it the only brand to buy. Products came from nowhere to become category leaders thanks to the strategy of the Unique Selling Proposition or USP.

Some of the brands that became famous utilizing the Reeves approach were Anacin, with its "fast, fast relief"; M&M candies "melts in your mouth not in your hands;" and Wonder Bread, supported with "builds strong bodies 12 ways." I understand the original claim was "8 ways," but somewhere along the line, Reeves thought 12 had a better ring to it and somehow found 4 more.

Reeves was not the founder of comparative advertising. However, his timing was such that the new medium of TV offered the perfect platform for the demonstration or side-by-side comparison. He was also a great proponent of the notion that frequency sells, and he utilized spot TV to advance this belief. The rest is advertising history.

The Benefits Sell

David Ogilvy, the crown prince of image advertising, did not develop this approach at the expense of selling the product. Ogilvy believed in selling; he claims to have learned about it from earning a living as a door-to-door salesman. He later learned more about consumers and their attitudes by working as a researcher for the Gallup organization of polling fame. After becoming a success, he advised all would-be copywriters to get Direct Response experience before venturing onto Madison Avenue. He learned much about people and he discovered how to put that knowledge to work by creating effective advertising— advertising that sold.

Mr. Ogilvy and Mr. Reeves believed in selling. And like many sales people, they knew what the basics were all about. They just came at the sales pitch from different angles. Reeves was "features" oriented and Ogilvy believed in conveying the "benefits" story. With one, the product was the hero, and the other attempted to establish a perceived consumer benefit. The benefit was supposed to provide the audience with a belief that their lives would be made better as a result of using this product.

Ogilvy convinced men that if they dressed in a Hathaway shirt, they would stand out as the man with the eye patch did in the ads. Women bought the shirts and men were happy to wear them. Commander Whitehead symbolized the exclusive British drawing-room appeal for the premium-priced Schweppes tonic water and club soda. The premium image was supported with the product claim that tiny bubbles delivered a benefit. People of culture wouldn't think of serving anything less than Schweppes. Dove soap was different from other facial bars since it contained one-quarter moisturizing cream. Women believed that this ingredient was beneficial to retain youthful looking skin. No soaps contained it because this would make the product too expensive. Ogilvy knew price would not stand in the way of beauty. He announced Dove's secret ingredient and demonstrated on TV how daily usage was the way to have beautiful skin thanks to the moisturizing cream. It worked, Dove carved out a significant share of the facial bar market held by Proctor & Gamble's Camay and Lever's sister brand Lux. Today, Dove is still a category leader and still uses the one-quarter moisturizing cream claim because Ogilvy knew that this promise offered the hope women wanted, and this promise still works today.

The Personality Sell

Leo Burnett was the creator of more personality icons than anyone in the history of advertising. He knew how to make friends with people and at the same time make a product come alive through the clever use of a fantasy character. If a live spokesperson, even a celebrity, was hawking a product, consumers might easily tune them out, but a cartoon character was not threatening. Often, the character was intriguing and friendly.

Enough so that, combined with a live photo or footage of the product in use, consumers could find themselves relating to the product in a simple child-like manner. The Chicago based Burnett was a different breed from the slick New York ad types; he had a more simple and humble approach to the selling process.

Most importantly, Burnett knew how to position a product in a friendly manner. As a result, people were happy to put the product in their shopping carts and welcome it into their homes as one would with a friend. This is the essence of creating a true product personality. Of course, not all of Burnett's ads used cartoon icons, but we seem to remember them best: the Green Giant, Tony the Tiger (plus a number of others for Kellogg's), and Charlie the Tuna. The appeal of these characters as product endorsers worked for adults, children and the kids within all of us. Therefore, they've stood the test of time, as has the Burnett agency.

The Soft Sell

Bill Bernbach was dubbed the creator of the soft sell. He is the final example I'll use to demonstrate the major contributions that these industry greats have made and how they have shaped the manner in which advertising is done today. Bernbach, in many ways, was the anti-ad man. He shifted away from the obvious and the traditional and he was not a great supporter of quantitative research. He liked the creative people to drive the process rather than have the account executives tell them what to do. He also instituted the concept of creative teams: a writer and art director working together, as opposed to the old way of having the writer develop the idea and the art director simply execute it. Of course, the growth of the TV medium helped this approach catch on throughout the ad industry.

Bernbach was a pragmatist, if not a salesman. He carried a note in his pocket that read, "maybe he's right." This philosophy was undoubtedly extended to include consumers. With a little paraphrasing it could say, "maybe they're not stupid, maybe you don't have to talk down to them, maybe I should understate rather than oversell."

Bernbach had a passion for pushing his advertising in this soft-sell direction. His passion was to be seen and felt in everything his company produced. His work resonated with his peers and registered with consumers. Somehow his undersell, underdog and under promise was a breath of fresh air to Americans who had been overpowered by the ad wars, which heated up with the advent of television advertising. His ads quietly moved consumers from the inside out rather than most messages that tried to attack from the outside and force their way in. He was the master of passive persuasion.

You'll remember the Alka Seltzer series that said little about how the product performed, but spent most of the time dwelling on the joys of overeating and the resulting indigestion. People laughed, identified with the problem and bought the product. Avis was an "also ran" in the car rental business, along came the "we're only #2, so we try harder" campaign and sales soared. And who could forget the introduction of the Volkswagen to the United States with ad headlines like "think small" and "Lemon" or commercials about "keeping up with the Jones." Bernbach's style of advertising is still considered a viable approach even in this day and age.

Reach the Boomers with Golden Oldies

The point is that these are four different but effective styles of advertising that the early Boomers cut their teeth on—figuratively, if not literally. All of the approaches described above were part of the driving force of the golden days of television in the late 50s through the late 70s. These were the formative years for the first wave of Boomers. They were 5 to 10 years old when these golden days started, and making their own buying decisions as it ended. The products and the advertising of that period are forever part of the maturation process of today's 50+ consumers. What worked then can still influence these Cutting-Edge Boomers now. We can combine the things we know about the 50+ consumer with the disciplines taught by Messers, Reeves, Ogilvy, Burnett and Bernbach. A wise application of advertising history might save us from having to repeat the process of learning these essential truths.

If your goal is to develop advertising which can't be ignored, is meaningful, memorable and motivates the consumer to take action, then it's time to revisit the basic components of the sale, and overlay these with the principles we gleaned from the giants of advertising. By carefully considering these truths, we should find a clear path to follow in an effort to effectively communicate with the 50+ segment of the Boomer market.

Chapter 9

Basic Sales Techniques Create Better Advertising

From the greats of advertising we have learned that discipline leads to success. Each of the men profiled in the previous chapter were students of advertising. They learned from the earlier greats—the Webs, the Rubicams, the Laskers—and applied this knowledge to develop and perfect their own rules. Yes the rules are necessary. They are not there to impede creativity or strategic thinking. Rather, the rules set the stage from which great advertising can be launched. Of course the rules can be broken, but must never be ignored; something many young ad people don't understand or accept.

For the sake of discussion, I've tried to take the one cogent point from what was my understanding of the philosophy of Reeves, Ogilvy, Burnett and Bernbach and make it part of a four-step equation to follow each time the creative process begins. It's difficult, if not presumptuous, to try and synthesize the disciplines of these industry giants into a few words or even a couple of sentences. This is not gospel, just one man's attempt to get his arms around the art of advertising and simplify it to a science—albeit inexact. Maybe by stating it here, you'll be encouraged to rethink your own disciplines and develop a more personalized set of rules, or "guidelines" to more effective advertising. You might have a different group of heroes but that doesn't matter. Truth is truth even though it might be relayed in a different manner.

Before tackling this task, it's appropriate to take a couple of minutes to review the selling process. If we agree that the advertising role is to sell something, then we must embrace or at least understand the principles of the selling proposition. If you are unwilling to accept the cold hard fact that selling isn't a dirty word, then don't ever get into a discussion about this concept with your CEO.

The Principles of Selling

There is an age-old formula used to describe the steps involved in a successful sale. It's not the only one; it is, however, the simplistic "AIDA" formula, which is the acronym for:

- A Attention

- I Interest

- D Desire

- A Action

These four words capture the elements of the entire sales process. Nothing has been left out, nothing needs to be added. We will focus on a face-to-face selling situation for now and look at each of the stages.

Attention is crucial because you must divert the prospect from whatever was on their mind and make them focus on what you have to say. Look at it as resetting their agenda. This phase should be short and sweet, otherwise their minds will wander and you'll lose them.

Interest in what you are saying keeps them on your agenda. "What's in it for me" must be addressed early in the pitch and throughout the process. Product features, even general benefits, won't garner their involvement and participation if you don't keep them interested.

Desire turns the prospect's attitude toward the product from a possible "need to have" into a "must have." This desire can be better accomplished by knowing as much as possible about the wants of the prospect than by expressing how the product satisfies them. Asking questions is a simple way to gather this information and invoking positive responses is an indication of how ready they are to buy.

Action is the step that only the prospect can take. You can lead them to it and motivate them in numerous ways, but you cannot make them buy. Using all the techniques of trial closes, or the famous ABCs of "always be closing," can only place you at the brink of the sale. Yet in a face-to-face sales situation, you instinctively know when you've arrived at the moment of truth: the instance when you ask for the order and shut up. At this point, the person who breaks the silence has bought into the other's proposition.

The entire sales process has just been summarized; there is nothing else. Yes, there are a lot of books on prospecting, overcoming objections, suggestive selling, and all kinds of techniques, and these techniques are great for improving your methodology and perfecting elements of the pitch. Yet none of these add to or subtract from the AIDA principle. Try it and you'll see that it's true. Speaking of truths, the above discussion dealt with face-to-face selling. Now try applying the truths of AIDA to the development of effective ads and commercials. It works because advertising's job is to sell!

Four Ways to Better Advertising

Let me return to the four icons of modern day advertising and how drawing on what we learned from each of them can be molded into a four-point approach to advertising, which complements the four-step AIDA formula.

- Point-of differentiation demonstrates how your product is unique from the competition. (Rosser Reeves would have addressed this through his USP.)

- Perceived benefit relates how your product will improve the life of the person using it. (David Ogilvy may have written detailed copy and used symbolic images to tell consumers why they should buy.)

- Product personality gives the consumer a reason to invite your product into their home. (Leo Burnett might have created a character to accomplish this.)

- Positive persuasion suggests that we don't over promise or overwhelm the consumer because if we address the other steps properly, we don't have to oversell. (Bill Bernbach could disarm skeptical consumers with a simple depiction of what to expect from the product by relating to them in an honest, understated way.)

These are the four Ps. Discover how they work in tandem with AIDA. Now see how your advertising measures up to them. Apply these approaches in the development of your next positioning statement or creative brief. You'll be surprised how focusing on the sale and the elements of the presentation can improve the effectiveness of your advertising, in general and particularly when its directed to the 50+ consumer.

Chapter 10

Mix Old and New Media for Success

New or improved distribution considerations may become viable alternatives in the coming years. Boomers will be at the forefront of the successful growth of these methods. Some of these considerations have been part of the distribution mode for years, while others are a new variation resulting from technology. Either way, they deserve to be discussed.

Catalogs and other mail-order businesses have been around for more than one hundred years. Originally, they gave rural Americans access to a vast array of general merchandise. Today, these vehicles offer people, who are not living in a location convenient to certain stores or do not have time to get to the stores, an opportunity to have the product delivered. This mode of distribution has become an effective means of offering specialty and lifestyle merchandise to a national audience. Busy 50+ Boomers are a prime audience with the experience to make shopping by mail an easy and satisfying alternative. Based upon the response rates reported by a number of Direct Response (DR) clients, it is estimated that this type of business accounts for less than three percent of total retail sales (*Response* Magazine, 2001), but it is disproportionately higher with the 50+ consumer. To appreciate the importance of how DR can work as part of a selling strategy, it is now appropriate to stop and review how e-commerce started, then stalled, and is now making a comeback.

If We Don't Learn from History, We're Doomed to Repeat It

Less than a decade ago the advent of the Internet and the e-commerce version of the catalog and direct-mail business exploded on the scene with the introduction of the dot com business model. According to the founders of these businesses and people rushing to invest their money in these unproven enterprises, this was the wave of the future. They seemed to believe that nobody was going to shop at retail stores anymore and that conventional shopping would become passé. They hoped that consumers were going to stay locked away in their rooms and order tons of merchandise as they clicked from website to website.

It didn't work out quite that way. It turned out that there really wasn't a viable ongoing business for most of these upstart companies. Consumer acceptance had not caught up with technology, so the dot com dream was in reality a nightmare. It had no real business foundation on which to build. Billions were spent on awareness advertising or "branding," as they liked to call it. Consumers were asked to log on to a website, which promised little or no apparent benefit to them, and once those who did visit the sites arrived, the infrastructure was not marketing oriented or consumer friendly. If a person did buy, delivery and after-sale service problems abounded. No wonder so many of these virtual firms dropped like flies.

The real problem was everyone started to believe their own PR and bought into the web marketing concept before it was road tested. A mob mentality prevailed and people were ready to make a killing by investing in dot com companies. Young technophiles, who had dropped out of college, were becoming multi-millionaires overnight. As new stock offerings appeared, the initial stock was gobbled up sooner than you could log on to the company's website. Nobody wanted to be left behind, so money kept pouring in, stock prices increased and few questioned the future of e-commerce.

Because sales were slow to materialize and profits were nonexistent, many of these firms could not continue to stay in business after the first or second round of funding ran out. They needed the infusion of additional money and a lot of it. The people running the companies recruited proven professionals from traditional businesses to help tame the tiger they held by the tail. Maybe investors had an enlightening when they thought about the traditional stocks they had purchased based on price earnings ratios. The past performance of a company and the experience of its management, hard assets, distribution, and consumer confidence all meant something, as opposed to discussing the *burn rate*, which is a term used to project how long a firm could keep spending at the current level before running out of money. The bubble burst and the investors took the hit, many people lost jobs and the consumers continued most of their personal business the old-fashioned way.

We all got excited about e-commerce. Consumers got connected and many experienced the potential convenience of doing business online. During the first big holiday shopping period, e-commerce accounted for about one percent of retail sales as reported by The Department of Commerce. Internet sales were about one third of the volume generated by catalog marketers. What's amazing is it took one category a hundred years to get there while the other did it in about a year. It tells us that there is a real e-commerce opportunity waiting to be developed, but only if it's managed and marketed effectively.

Who is going to be the driving force behind the next phase of Internet marketing? You guessed it—the 50+ Boomers, and here's why. The early adopters of the Internet were mostly young people and technophiles. However, these were not the people who bought a major share of traditional goods and services, and they were not convinced by the e-commerce marketers to change their buying habits. When young families started to become interested in buying goods and services online, most Internet companies were not prepared to handle the demands of such business. This resulted in problems that became expediential, thereby hastening the demise of many businesses not equipped for the long battle to attain marketing supremacy.

What many companies came to understand, except in a few instances, was that the Internet was not an end in itself; it was merely a means to an end. For the most part, it is not to be used instead of other modes of communications or distribution, but rather in concert with them. That's why brick and mortar is interchangeable with brick and click, not in lieu of it. Current mainstream retailers will be able to have their cake and eat it too if they're willing to build their business on the rubble that many dot com firms left behind. Consumers have had a taste of doing business through the Net, now give them what they want, actively promote the benefits and they will come.

Put E-Commerce and Direct Response in Your Tool Kit

Why do I say the Boomers are the answer to e-commerce? Let us return to the fact that they are the experienced shoppers. They have learned the basics of computers and will combine this with their need for information and their understanding of catalog shopping along with traditional retail shopping. Expect them to go online for hard-to-find or specialty items. They will also use it to help make the buying decisions on considered purchases then go to a retailer to consummate the sale. But do not look for them to buy commodity or many impulse products online or to navigate a website for a service that they are already familiar with. Do look for them to make more and more online purchases where they used to order by phone, mail or fax. In the meantime, the younger people will be expanding their e-commerce purchases as they continue to mature as consumers. But for now, the ones who will make the Internet the marketing powerhouse it deserves to be are the Boomers, particularly the 50+ Boomers.

So what is the role of the Internet in marketing? Is it a medium or a means of distribution? It is both, however, the emphasis swings depending on what is being marketed and to whom. Those younger than the 50+ Boomers use the Internet as an alternative to letter writing, phone calls and news gathering, while Cutting-Edge Boomers use traditional methods to accomplish the same tasks. Therefore, online advertising can be effective for one group and not for the other. However, it is a distribution channel for virtually any group. That's where the short-term profit opportunities exist.

Direct Response advertisers are seeing 25 even 35 percent of their sales coming to them via the Internet as opposed to the standard toll-free numbers (Direct Marketing Association, August 1999). This suggests that every advertiser, whether engaged in a branding effort or a direct sale, ought to include their website address in all ads and commercials. Smart brand builders will have their phone numbers displayed as well, and they'll encourage consumers to contact them for more information. This gives marketers an opportunity to build a relationship, capture the consumer's name, and maybe even sell something anytime a consumer contacts them. Once the name is in the data bank, true relationship marketing can be an ongoing tactic.

Other favorable results of the online response are the relative low cost of operation and the control the marketers have in terms of the information disseminated. The good news is the human factor has been eliminated. The bad news is the human factor has been eliminated. People generally want to talk with another person when they have questions. However, they would rather not have the personal contact if they think it could end up in a sales pitch. From a marketer's point of view, not having operators standing by saves money and mistakes. Yet few websites can anticipate when consumer resistance will come into play or can answer objections in a way that will result in getting the order. Technology will advance the home-page sales pitch and bring in a live person at the appropriate time to tie-up the order. Therefore, the more you use the Internet as a sales tool now, the more capable you'll become at using it. This optimizes how the Net will serve you as a future distribution tool.

The Internet can be a cheaper way to sell direct than through multi-level distribution, provided that the product has a selling price that significantly exceeds the cost of shipping and handling and there are no major gaps in your distribution network. Otherwise, you can use the Net as a tool to direct the consumer to selected retailers. Besides, there are many consumers who like to go out to shop and consider it a way to get away from the stress of every day activities. Use online coupons and other inducements to get them to the stores, then direct your efforts back to the retailers in order to gain their support. The crossover opportunities are endless.

There is no reason why marketers should not be selling consumers through every possible mode of distribution. The Internet may provide a safe means to do this because the concept has been around for years. For instance, Sears sells all kinds of tools through their Direct Response TV spots. Usually it's one tool that performs a multitude of tasks for a low price plus shipping and handling. If industry standards apply, for every piece sold directly through the commercial another ten or more will be sold at a Sears retail outlet. Why aren't more retailers and manufacturers taking a page from the Sears approach?

It is estimated by some industry practitioners that less than 10 percent of the people in this country have ever bought a product or service through a Direct Response vehicle. Based on results I have seen, those who respond are generally 50 years of age or older. As the Boomers continue to age there will be more and more opportunities to sell to them on a direct basis, where you control everything from the message to the pricing to getting the item into their hands. You don't have the sales expenses, slotting allowances, or promotional costs that whittle down your profits. However, if you already have the retail channels in place, you can capture those who will buy direct and leave the rest for the retailer.

Now don't get all huffy and complain that this robs you of business if you're a retailer. For years the marketers have built their respective categories and turned the business over to retailers. The marketer advertises and creates demand. When the potential customer comes into a store looking for the branded product, a switch is attempted at the point of sale based on the price of similar private-label merchandise. It doesn't matter whether it's dishwashing liquid, refrigerators or house paint, every retailer does it. So let the manufacturer get some of the gravy. With the Direct Response approach, they'll still be driving

10 times the business your way. If you are a manufacturer, get out there now and capture a share of the direct business that's waiting for you. Get those millions of Boomers who are 50+ now, and get ready for the tens of millions more on the way.

Branding and Direct Response Can Work Together

The next logical question is "can I do branding and Direct Response simultaneously or does it take a separate effort?" The answer is a bit complex. If your branding effort ignores those over 50, then chances are you'll be starting from scratch. However, if you have a message that appeals to this audience, then reworking or adding on to what you're already doing may do the trick.

Let's examine this a little closer. Direct Response advertising, by its very nature, has to evoke immediate action. With broadcast DR, if the phone calls don't come in within 10 minutes of the time that the program ran, they often won't be coming in at all. Because the response is so immediate, most advertisers rely on banks of operators to handle the flood of calls. Then all is quiet until the next commercial or infomercial runs. Unless these ads move the consumer to take action immediately, the ads do not deliver results. A proven approach to accomplish results is through the use of the already discussed AIDA formula: Attention, Interest, Desire, Action. These steps are followed by successful salesmen, and it is also a sure-fire way to build a successful DR ad.

Unfortunately, most branding ads do not complete the AIDA equation. The efforts seem to assume that consumers will, after time, remember the brand name when it's time to purchase the product or service. This seems to be opposed to sound marketing principles. Entertaining or subliminal ads are often a disservice to the marketer because the message is so soft that it forgets to sell. These ads do not establish how the product or service is unique, nor do they provide the perceived benefits, which show how the product will improve the user's life.

I am not suggesting that branding efforts be abandoned, or that you change everything to a Direct Response model. Marketing is a process, and advertising results may not always be immediate. Success is not simply determined by the number of calls received. What I am trying to say is the consumer, particularly the mature consumer, might make a decision faster and take action sooner if you use DR strategies and tactics to educate and motivate them. Much of the media used for DR purposes differs from what you are already scheduling, so there is little to lose and much to gain by testing this approach.

Test, Test, Test

The key to DR success is test and measure; then adjust and test and measure again. The process is continuous. This applies to the strategies used and the creative approach, as well as the media selected to carry the message. Offers and price points must also be considered along with how the items being offered are bundled. Set aside some of your budget to test these variables with enough weight behind them to determine what works and what does not. Done properly, the marketing budget will continually regenerate itself through its own contributions.

You'll also want to look at things like taking an existing 30-second TV spot, that talks to the 50+ audience, and adding a 30-second DR spot to it. This piggyback 60 second commercial could then run at Direct Response rates in appropriate DR time slots on networks where you would not normally place your general branding advertising. If the commercial is successful, you have accomplished branding and response at the same time.

Then you might develop a completely new DR version to integrate your brand personality with the direct sell into a single commercial.

As stated, normally the DR media mix is different from the branding media plan. First you can not be obsessed with reach and frequency, but rather focus on the kinds of stations and programs that give you the right atmosphere to garner a response. Primetime, first run shows won't do it, nor do live action events or fast-moving sporting activities, because the programming overshadows the product. Alternative primetime, daytime, late night and weekend programming, including syndicated shows as well as reruns are good DR considerations. In addition, radio news and talk shows will consistently create a response. These are just some of the differences you will consider as you test a DR effort aimed at the older Boomer market.

Now let's return to the possibility of using the Direct Response model to support a retail-oriented business as stated earlier. Using a toll-free number and a website allows you to capture names and direct consumers to the nearest retailer, as well as provide the consumer with a coupon or other incentive to buy the product on their next store visit. This approach also allows the marketer to consider ways of making additional sales. The person who calls or logs on already has more than a passing interest in the product or service. So what enticement can you offer? Let's say it's a food product. Recipes and serving suggestions would be an idea; send them the materials or have them download it. Newsletters also help build a relationship. If you're trying to reach the 50+ market, nutritional information is an important part of what you might provide. Cross-selling with other manufacturers or selected retailers can help defray the costs, and it will garner cooperation from them. Sweepstakes, recipe contests and any other method for encouraging response will go a long way in building your relationship with the mature consumer. Once this is established, you can enlist their help through a tell-a-friend effort or a request for names of people who may like receiving information and samples of your products. Today's tech marketers call this "viral marketing;" "tell-a-friend" seems less threatening and personal. Be sure to reward the customer for their help and loyalty on a regular basis with coupons and other incentives.

Using Infomercials to Sell Non-Direct Response Products

Back in the late 80s when infomercials where revolutionizing the world of Direct Response advertising, I developed and produced a hybrid show concept, which combined the power of a half-hour program with the educational and relationship value of a cooking segment. These brand-specific cooking shows featured an experienced television and radio personality who was also the author of many cookbooks as the hostess. Each show spotlighted a single product and demonstrated how to use it to make delicious dishes for the family to enjoy.

It was a blended concept which provided the viewer with entertainment, information about a product category, the specific benefits of a particular brand, and instruction on how to use the products. It also offered free recipes and money-saving coupons by simply calling a toll-free number. Callers were also offered cookbooks and videotapes at nominal prices. Response was generated during the ordering opportunities between segments of the show. Once their names were secured, newsletters and promotional materials including coupons were sent to the consumer on a regular basis, usually quarterly. Cross-promotions were shared by the participating sponsors to reduce costs and allow them to have access to an audience that had a proven affinity to these programs.

The programs could be scheduled nationally, locally or within a specific cable-system's coverage area. This allowed the show sponsors to cast a broad net or target specific marketing areas. The food brokers pre-sold the supermarkets on tying in with the show by displaying the feature brands along with the meats and produce needed to make the recipes. Tear-off pads promoted the recipes and gave those who didn't order a chance to respond. Once the show's time slots were determined, they were advertised in the local TV guide and/or in the daily TV listings of the newspaper. It was a complete turnkey package.

These brand-specific cooking shows made the rounds for a couple of years before we stopped airing them. With more non-DR advertisers getting into the infomercial arena and aggressive spending by those already committed to this form of marketing, it became inefficient to continue expanding the concept. However, for a time, these programs made some brands famous with selective audiences, built relationships with them, created a buzz among consumers and generated greater trade support while baffling competitors. Maybe it's time to revisit this concept and marry it to a website, making it more efficient than using phone operators and mailing materials to consumers.

Word-of-mouth advertising has proven to be effective for all kinds of consumables and durables as well as a variety of services including financial and even funeral planning. It all starts, however, when someone gets excited enough to call or click on a product or service, even though they wouldn't normally expect to take this kind of action. You piqued their interest, now they're looking to you for help. By providing this help in an appropriate and timely manner, you have started to build a relationship of trust. The mature consumer appreciates a relationship established on trust and you become a friend in a sea of faceless products and services. This can help turn a casual or moderate user into a loyal user once they become comfortable with the product. If they are given help, they will discover more applications for it so they could turn into heavy users. Not only do the Boomers provide you with potential long-term customers, each satisfied customer could bring you many more like them. Wouldn't it be considered a successful effort if you were the number-one seller of your products and services among the growing throng of 50+ Boomers?

Chapter 11

Supermarkets Must Provide what the 50+ Boomers Want

Eating is one of life's simple pleasures. We eat more in this country, both at home and away from home, than most other regions of the world. Food store volume, restaurant receipts and our waistlines all attest to that.

The Boomers have been the primary force in this development. This generation wanted for nothing. They weren't deprived of food because of the depression, nor did they experience rationing because of the food shortages caused by World War II. Food was definitely a part of their life. Many were raised on formula, not mother's milk, so prepared foods became a part of their existence early in life. Moms learned that TV was a good babysitter and that TV with food was even better. TV dinners, canned spaghetti, and boxed macaroni and cheese were served to children while they watched commercials, which suggested what else they could eat.

These are the same Boomers who welcomed fast food with open arms, and if they moved to a different part of their own city or around this vast country, there was always a McDonald's, Burger King, or Pizza Hut nearby. Although these weren't distinctive restaurants, the food was always consistent and convenient. The franchise operators loved a mobile populace. Standardization replaced regional tastes as the chains proliferated. The

Boomers moved around with apparent ease, even though it took a psychological toll. A good way to stuff the feelings was with food. That may explain why the United States produces more snack foods and desserts than any other country, and why American's waistlines continue to expand.

Pairing TV with food started early and has continued through the years for these 50+ Boomers. However, more Cutting-Edge Boomers are eating healthier and exercising today in an effort to look and feel good as they move into the second half of life. Nonetheless, convenience is still an important factor in the food choices they make.

With so many two-income families, time is always a factor. Even when they became Empty-Nesters the time element wasn't eliminated. Preparing dinner for two requires about the same amount of time as dinner for four. Going out to a restaurant takes less time than preparing a similar dish at home, and it is a pleasant and relaxing experience. With the children gone, there's also the opportunity for less regimentation in one's life. However, most Boomers have established their routines and tend to follow them—with children or not, with spouse or not.

Let's investigate some theories regarding what these Cutting-Edge Boomers want in terms of the products they buy, where they buy it and what their preparation and serving needs are at home as well as what factors are important when they eat out.

Food and the 50+ Boomer

The 50+ Boomer is now looking for a less complicated life. A fast-paced lifestyle is not as exciting as it once was. That doesn't mean that the Cutting-Edge Boomer will stop being busy, but it does mean that they want to stop being crazy. For the most part, the children are grown or gone and that automatically reduces the stress at home. Work is another matter. The electronic age hasn't made things easier; it just accelerated the process of communications. Pagers, cell phones, faxes, email and now personal digital assistants (PDAs) have made us accessible 24 hours a day, seven days a week. No wonder the stress level is over the top. These "conveniences" were not something the 50+ Boomer grew up with. Enjoying a leisurely meal away from the rat race is something the mature consumer savors.

Before enjoying a meal at home, one usually has to go shopping. That word isn't necessarily bad, however it does mean different things to men and women. For the ladies, shopping is generally associated with the pleasant task of looking for and buying clothes, or it could be choosing furniture or selecting a gift for or a loved one. Even the trip to the supermarket can connote the gathering of foods to be used to make delicious meals for all to enjoy. However, if one is short on time, it's an unpleasant chore to be completed as quickly as possible. That's the way it is for most trips to the supermarket for most ladies of the house. Men, on the other hand, view shopping as a kind of hunting expedition. If we are sent by our spouses, the tendency is to dash in, get whatever is on the list, pay little attention to the price and get through the checkout lines as quickly as possible. However, when we go to the store with our wives, which is as infrequently as possible, we take on the role of explorer and snatch up all the strange, exotic and expensive items that we can find and load them into the cart. Suddenly, time doesn't matter as long as we're getting what *we* want.

Supermarket operators have long been aware of these habits. They have always catered to the women and tried to accommodate the men. Product selection and placement, store temperature, the music played, and the width of aisles were all designed to make the experience as enjoyable as possible and slow down the pace a little because that allowed people more time to browse. There was a time when knowledge of the consumer was applied to better serve the customer, but now such information may just be a tool to improve the bottom line.

Not long ago, the grocery business was strictly a local business; there never was a truly national chain. There were some big regional and quasi-national operators, but nobody had a store distribution pattern that could be considered nationwide. Less than 20 years ago, there were many strong regional and local brands, which rivaled or outsold their national counterparts in selected markets. Store managers and district merchandisers had the discretion to stock products and expand shelf space to accommodate local brands requested by their customers. *Slotting allowances* and *category management* were terms that had not yet become part of the trade jargon.

Now the big guys are getting bigger. The three major players in the retail food business, Albertsons, Kroger and Safeway are increasing their market share in established markets by expansion and through acquisition. Some of the acquired stores operate under their better-known local name, but it won't be long before we see national supermarket chains dominating the marketplace. Wal-Mart and other mass merchants are already offering food through their network of stores. However, for the purpose of this discussion, I am referring to freestanding supermarket operators. Greater control over operations, coupled with increased buying power, resulting in better service and overall lower prices is a notion these giants would love the public to accept. Can these chains deliver on this promise and should the consumer believe it? Where might this concept fall short?

Supermarkets Have Forgotten what Business They're In

In the 1900s, grocers were purveyors of fresh foods, primarily meats and produce. As technology increased, processed foods and packaged goods of all descriptions were added to the retail mix. Corner stores later grew into supermarkets and moved from service to self-service. The perimeter of the store was considered to provide service such as meats and produce, then bakery and deli. Now the perimeter contains other take-out offerings including flowers, banking and more. The center of the store has been expanded to stock more frozen foods and more non-foods, plus ethnic and health food products. Club and warehouse competition has resulted in huge size/multi-pack sections and bigger stores have produced a "store within a store" concept such as a natural/healthy food store run by a specialist in this area. And, in larger metropolitan areas, many stores are open 24 hours a day, seven days a week.

Has all this change been good for the consumer thereby making it good for the supermarkets? Volume per square foot is up at about the same rate as inflation and profit is flat throughout the industry. This suggests people are having their needs met elsewhere. Clubs, warehouse stores and even mass merchants offer staples at lower prices. Some have better cuts of meats and fresher produce and seafood than the local supermarket, along with the lower prices. Not all consumers, especially the Cutting-Edge Boomers, need the quantities required by these low-price operators. They'll pay for service, but often they can't get it at the local supermarket. The chains have overlooked the obvious need to be merchants again. They switched roles with the manufacturers and are trying to be marketers, and it's not benefiting the consumer.

The role reversal came about at the same time slotting allow-ances came into vogue. Before that, the private label was always a way for the supermarket to compete with manufacturer's brands. The private label would sell for less and switch the price con-scious customer at the point-of-purchase. Slotting, however, put the squeeze on the manufacturer by forcing them to essentially buy the shelf space. In addition, they still had to support their brand through advertising and promotion. Smaller marketers and local brands couldn't compete, so many sold their label and distribution network to national marketers. The shelves took on a new appearance.

A couple of national brands, a price brand and a store brand made up most categories. Then came category management, which continued to put the squeeze on manufacturers. But with fewer players in the category, prices could be slowly escalated to offset the cost of allowances for the marketer and still deliver profit to the chains. With brands increasing their prices, private-label prices could be raised too, as long as a favorable difference could be maintained. Who paid the price—the consumer of course.

While this is going on at the core of the store, more self-ser-vice and less personal service is happening at the perimeter. At the service counters in many stores, there's no one to help cus-tomers in the evenings; no meat manager in the meat depart-ment; no baker in the bakery department; and no produce man-ager in the produce department. Don't the stores know this is when most working people have to shop? With stores that have similar quality (including cleanliness, selection and personnel) and generally competitive prices, service is the only thing that will separate one store's value from another. The 50+ consumer may be the only customer who is willing to pay more for service, and when doing so, they actually believe the value is greater.

That's right, Cutting-Edge Boomers will gladly pay more for service and come away with a feeling of greater value.

Let's go back to the first part of the equation and take a look at where quality fits in, especially with the Cutting-Edge Boomers. Selection is an important part of quality and the customer wants to be in control of their purchasing decisions. Having choices means having it their way. Before the Boomers were consumers, the biggest supermarket chain was the Great Atlantic and Pacific Tea Company (A&P). They had about 3,000 stores scattered throughout major cities primarily east of Mississippi with the greatest concentration being in the Northeast. A&P may have been the first chain to promote a private label with coffee and tea carrying their name.

By the late 50s and early 60s, A&P had proliferated their private-label business by offering three price levels in most major food categories, be it canned, boxed or frozen. This good, better, best concept is not new. It has been effective as a means of trading consumers up in price in the past and it still works. A&P offered Iona as the price line, then Sultana in the middle, with Ann Page (A&P) at the top end. The only problem was that the consumer didn't relate these private labels to the quality of the manufacturer's brands. They thought they weren't as good, and although lower in price the value was not positively perceived. This translated to A&P's quality image diminishing with fewer people buying their brand and more people shopping elsewhere. It was once the largest supermarket chain in the United States but there are no A&P stores today.

Has the modern supermarket chain operator learned from this quality-perception story? I think not. They believe they control the real estate so it's up to them to parcel it out as they choose. This kind of arrogance is also apparent in the way they cut back on service to meet their bottom-line requirements. That leaves them with price as their main attribute, something they really can't compete on and if they did it would surely devastate their bottom line. So these retailers claim to offer value instead of low price while ignoring the main factors which contribute to this perception: quality and service. They choose not to go back to the basics of being merchants and to leave marketing to the marketing people. Therefore, you can expect them to continue selling shelf space and programs to the manufacturers while trying to build their own brands with consumers. And it's the consumer who ends up paying higher prices and getting less for what they spend.

The understanding of what has taken place in the supermarket business, which is arguably the most competitive retail battlefield known to marketers, is important to everyone engaged in commerce. Seeing how distribution has overshadowed the dominion of the brand, coupled with the rise and fall and rise again of private-label merchandise, is not a matter regularly discussed by most 50+ Boomers. Yet they lived through these cycles as discernable consumers worth being targeted by both marketers and retailers alike.

Will the manufacturer produce and promote products specifically designed to appeal to the 50+ Boomer? Or will the supermarkets start providing and promoting services especially for the Boomers? Someone has to make the first move. Those who are not involved with this class of business can learn a great deal about what motivates the Cutting-Edge Boomers by observing the activities that could be heating up at the supermarket level in the near future.

Chapter 12

How to Bring 50+ Boomers Back to the Supermarket

If marketers are in touch and in tune with the consumers, I believe they can regain the control of the marketing process. Many already have by selling to the clubs and warehouse stores as alternative modes of distribution. Although this began in a sly way, by packing industrial or food service sizes in multi-unit, overwrapped packages, this form of retailing has since become legitimate, and some of the variations have even made their way onto supermarket shelves.

One step that will directly benefit the supermarkets, and provide them with an advantage over the encroaching alternative outlets, is learning how to cash in on the Cutting-Edge Boomer. First, a marketer must revisit the product line and evaluate where the marketing emphasis has been placed. Marketers must not only look at what might appeal to the 50 to 55 year old consumer, but also consider those in the Swing Generation, ages 55 to 65. Together they make up the super-spender group of Empty-Nesters. They are blessed with plenty of disposable income because virtually all of them are still working yet they have reduced debt responsibilities. If you offer the products, which do or could appeal to them, then you're about to strike oil.

It's not just the big guys, like Heinz, Campbell or Kraft, who can tap into this market. Specialty products such as natural foods, even products that have been quiet for a while, as well as new products, have an opportunity to get a meaningful share of the waiting 50+ market. Many of the global packaged-goods marketers such as Lever Bros., and Proctor & Gamble have been reducing the number of stock keeping units (SKUs) in their worldwide product line up. Many stagnant or smaller brands have been or will be sold off to accomplish this strategic decision, yet some of them can still be a formidable force in marketing to the 50+ Boomers just through proper positioning, niche marketing and advertising. There are also smaller companies with committed management who are willing and able to target entire brands toward this burgeoning consumer segment. The key to success is to be the first to capture this market and be dedicated to keeping a hold on it as the remaining Boomers follow.

There are many examples of specialty products that have gone mainstream over the years. Many had ethnic origins such as Ramen noodles or salsa. Some came from a health-foods background like rice cakes and natural cereals. Others came from consumer demands such as "diet anything," while some took the premium product position. All have become complete categories or sections within today's supermarkets. Some of the original brands are still on top while others could use some rethinking in order to get back in the race.

Reach the Boomers with Old Favorites

One of the best-known quality brands in the grocer's freezer is Stouffer's. Their familiar coral-colored label started appearing in stores in the 1950s. It was positioned as a premium brand for premium tastes backed by the reputation of its restaurants on the East Coast and in the Mid West. The products were more sophisticated than typical frozen dinners and appealed more to a lifestyle rather than to a certain demographic. For instance, a low-paid assistant college professor might pay the premium price and enjoy a Stouffer's entrée with a side dish, while a trucker who earned twice as much would be happy with an inexpensive TV dinner. This product's sophisticated persona prevailed for years, and then the diet craze hit and Stouffer's introduced Lean Cuisine. Much of its marketing emphasis was put into the new line, which appealed to diet-conscious women. Naturally, when Lean Cuisine was brought into the frozen food case, the regular coral-colored package lost some facings. Later the original Stouffer's line got some new attention when macaroni & cheese and lasagna was introduced in the family pack (which can be found at clubs, warehouse stores, and supermarkets). This pack took up more space and the single entrée, and two-serving side dish items in the coral package were further reduced. Later, Hearty Lean Cuisine was launched to broaden the brand's appeal. The target audience was men and possibly women who did not want to lose weight. In any event, a look at the freezer shelf showed that the coral pack had lost more facings.

For some time I was convinced that Stouffer's should resurrect the famous coral package for the 50+ Boomer market. I thought Stouffer's should recognize that the smaller households with sophisticated taste—primarily the millions of Empty-Nest families—would represent a significant base of business that would grow over the next decade or two. Clearly, Lean Cuisine, Hearty Lean Cuisine, family packs and the other line extensions marketed under the Stouffer's brand were not normally purchased by the 50+ consumer. Much of the advertising for these products did not even reach the Cutting-Edge Boomer, and if it did, the message was often irrelevant. I reasoned that directing specific advertising to the 50+ consumer, by reminding them that Stouffer's was always their favorite and was right for their life-style, would be an appropriate way to capture this neglected consumer. As it turned out, Stouffer's obviously saw the need and took the concept one step further. In early 2002, I began to notice advertising for a new line: Stouffer's HomeStyle Entrees. The product offers an entree and a side dish in one package, and the advertising is tastefully aimed at the 50+ consumer with TV spots appearing in the programming that appeals to this group. HomeStyle Entrees complement and reinforce the positioning of the original coral package line. Nestle, the multi-national marketing giant who owns the Stouffer's brand, saw the wisdom of targeting the 50+ consumer and will certainly reap the rewards.

Good taste may bring one brand back and good health could increase the stature of others. People 50+ are the fastest growing group of exercisers (Fitness Council Survey, 1997) and are becoming more concerned about eating healthy. This is not necessarily to lose weight, although this is the goal of many, but to stay healthy for the long haul. Products with low sodium, lower fat and fewer chemicals should be brought to their attention. Healthy Choice created their concept superbly for all consumers and positioned their product next to category leaders on the shelf. In the freezer case, Healthy Choice offers a number of products and the brand has a sizable billboard display. You'll also find the bold green package in the cereal aisle where it has a different look from the other brands. It reminds shoppers that it's not like the other products on the shelf, so they should try it. The same is true in the meat section and every other place where the Healthy Choice brand has decided to compete. Plus its claim appeals to many demographic and psychographic segments. What a great strategy! I recently noticed television commercials for their soup line. The commercials direct the selling message at the 50+ consumer by employing actors who obviously are part of this age group and appear to be health conscious, active consumers.

Healthy Choice obviously knows who they want to reach and they've gone after them.

With the 50+ Boomers, there's room for other brands, other products and other categories. Consider adult drinks; would an easily prepared, good tasting, decaffeinated iced tea appeal to the Cutting-Edge Boomer and beyond? Is there a market for ready-to-eat salad for two with individual packets of low fat, but good tasting, dressing included? Go to the natural food section, the supplement section or the specialty food department and see what items could move to the mainstream sections and appeal to the 50+ consumer, as is or with a little re-engineering and some repositioning.

The one caveat, and it's a big one, is that good-for-you products must taste good in order to succeed. Too often I've heard people proclaim that when it came to healthy foods the box may be better tasting than the product. This is no joke for marketers. People will try a product based on the health claim, but repeat sales will be a result of the taste it delivers. Even though the consumer is willing to compromise somewhat for the apparent benefits a product offers, they will not totally give up taste. For the aging consumer, whose taste buds may be tiring, there is a need to deliver more flavor in their foods, so the promise of good taste must be a reality. Because it costs so much to create trial, it's vital to build a base of users who buy again and again. It's the only way to keep a position on the shelf and the only way to make a profit.

In the perimeter area of the stores, custom cuts of meat and repackaging in smaller portions will appeal to Empty-Nesters. In the produce section, half bundles of items like asparagus could be attractive to these consumers. In the bakery department, mini loaves of bread or desserts for two, or maybe some sugarless or fat-free items would sell because those consumers are hungry for comfort foods but also have an eye on their waistlines. And in the service deli, meal replacement items specifically designed for adult tastes, again with good health in mind and packaged together for two people, could capture the attention of those 50+. Inspired by some marketing done by the manufacturers and encouraged by the sales results, the stores themselves will undoubtedly jump on the Cutting-Edge Boomer bandwagon.

With 30,000 or more items carried by the average super-market, there's absolutely no reason why an application for the 50+ Boomer can't be found in every department in the store, in virtually every aisle and in most categories.

Learn More About what the Cutting-Edge Boomers Want and Why

Once the products have been identified, compare your products with those of competitors, some of which are known to be 50+ Boomer friendly. Conduct a series of focus group sessions with consumers, and use discussions about the products as a way to learn what these Cutting-Edge Boomers think. You can discuss a whole host of subjects to learn their desires and preferences and how these affect the way this audience responds in their choice of goods and services.

Here's a little trick you might use to learn about the Cutting-Edge Boomer; it's a technique we use regularly at my ad agency. Take a video camera to places where you'll find people aged 50 to 55 such as malls, supermarket parking lots, and even churches after services are over. Approach the people you want to learn about and have a short list of questions prepared to keep the interviews on track. Then talk with as many people as possible. You'll find that once they become comfortable being on camera, these folks will generally talk well beyond the questions posed and get into great detail about the subject matter. The presence of the camera makes them feel important and they're more willing to provide you with in-depth and personal information. The interviews are reviewed by the account team then edited to provide an overview. The interviews are shown to all agency support groups as well as the client's marketing communications people. Often, before presenting positioning briefs, we prepare the discussion with a review of the taped interviews. It's also a useful tool to use as a prelude to presenting an ad campaign to the client's sales force. There are many useful ways to use reactions from people on the street, so I suggest that you investigate how to adopt this tool to learn what the Cutting-Edge Boomers have to say.

Knowing what triggers the selection process for the impulse items, as well as considered purchases, will help you understand the scale on which decisions are made. The more you understand what motivates or turns off these seasoned buyers, the better you'll be able to serve them. And the more they feel that you are serving them, the better you'll do in terms of building a Cutting-Edge Boomer business.

Perhaps the product you're currently marketing fits right into the 50+ Boomer's lifestyle, with virtually no changes required. Just remember that promotions and advertising must still be designed for and directed to this specific audience. Price is not necessarily the key purchasing motivation, but some other reward may be more appropriate, and therefore more effective in generating consumer response. A small percentage of sales donated to a camp promotion, which helps underprivileged children attend a summer camp, may tip the scales in favor of one product over another. Why? Because the Cutting-Edge Boomers still have a social conscience, and this particular promotion allows them to exercise it without changing their lives or involving their precious time. Be sure the "cause" is one that this audience can and will relate to enough in order to support the purchase decision. You might want to consider putting a discount on the larger sizes and restrict the camp offer to the size most likely to be purchased by the 50+ consumer. That way the actual point of purchase is the place where the audience can be differentiated. However, be sure you know which consumer is most likely to buy the various sizes in order to match the product and promotion with the proper people. Unfortunately, price conscious younger consumer, will be more motivated by a discount than the more altruistic camp promotion. Different appeals will undoubtedly require different approaches to communicate their messages.

As you become more adept at identifying the similarities of the 50+ Boomers with those who are younger, you can then determine what differences really count when it relates to buying considerations. An entire new world of marketing opportunities can be available to you, both now and in the years to come.

You don't have to reinvent the wheel. Many products that could serve the needs of the Cutting-Edge Boomers are already on the shelves, are being sold through other retail outlets or are being marketed directly to the consumer. However, size, nutrition, and positioning may have to be adjusted before these products are ready to be reintroduced to the 50+ consumers. Testing will quickly tell you what changes should be made. Of course, if you've developed a break-through product designed specifically for the 50+ Boomers, confirm through research that it delivers meaningful benefits. Then you can roll out your brand with the support it deserves and with the assurance that these consumers will buy it.

Chapter 13

SNAKE OIL, VIAGRA AND DIRECT MARKETING

Going directly to the consumer is a relatively new marketing technique in the prescription drug field, but the concept got its start in the dawn of modern advertising history. Patent medicines were the evolutionary step from "snake oils." In fact, some of the early successes in modern medicine got their initial distribution from the back of a road-show wagon. These potions were good for everything from headaches to hemorrhoids to bunions and everything in between. Often, one of these magic elixirs cured a wide variety of ailments. However, with the advent of print advertising, came market segmentation and product positioning. Cure-alls found they could differentiate themselves from the competition by narrowing their claims and concentrating on how they thought their product performed best.

Advertising was the vehicle that these entrepreneurs used to sell their products. Newspapers, and the magazines that followed, were jammed with small-space direct-response ads for salves, tonics and jars of creams which claimed, if ordered immediately and used regularly, would take care of whatever health problem the consumer bought it to cure.

Some marketers sought distribution through pharmacies in their hometowns and advertised on a Direct Response basis to areas where they had no distribution. Some pharmacists concocted their own products and sold it to their own customers before broadening distribution and commencing to advertise. Even one of the most powerful brands of our time, Coca Cola, started life in a drug store. This fountain syrup became a "pick-me-up" tonic, starting its career in Atlanta almost a century ago, before becoming the world's favorite soft drink.

Over the years, government regulations restricted the claims made by manufacturers and determined what products could be sold over-the-counter (OTC) and which ones could only be sold through prescription. Prescription drugs became known as ethical drugs, and as such they did not advertise to the consumer. People only heard of them from their doctors because people trusted what the doctor said, not what a marketer promoted. Why didn't anyone think to ask the doctors how they learned about new drugs?

The answer, of course, was kept quiet. Once an M.D. left medical school the information reached him through journals, which included editorials with the information often provided by the pharmaceutical people with ads paid for by them. In addition, hordes of "detail salesmen" were dispensed by these companies to explain directly to doctors why they should prescribe the drugs that the firm manufactured. Before the salesmen left the offices, the doctors were loaded up with samples, prescription pads that carried a product name and promotional literature which told patients why their doctor was recommending this particular drug. If it was a "hot" drug, these pieces of advertising often found their way into the waiting room, so the patient could be pre-sold before being given the prescription. That's how the ethical drug people did it then and still do it now.

In the meantime, Anacin, Carter's Liver Pills, Doan's Backache Pills and a myriad of other OTC products keep hammering away at the consumer through advertising. As a result, consumers were conditioned to believe that they were empowered to diagnose minor physical problems and prescribe their own treatment. If one product didn't provide relief then they'd simply switch to another brand. Although the ethical drug manufacturers produced many of the OTC products, they were able to coexist by one being on the shelf in the front of the store and the other in the back behind the pharmacist's counter. Consumer advertising was for the OTC brands, while the important, reliable drugs were backed by a doctor's recommendation.

Until the early 1900s, there were different schools of medicine. These included homeopathic, osteopathic, and others. However, under the AMA one school of thought was embraced; it was the popular position in Europe as well. Modern Western medicine became the standard practice. This was the established medical system for 50 years and people didn't think much about changing things. Suddenly the Cutting-Edge Boomers, who were young at the time, came along and questioned anything that was part of the establishment. So for the past 30 or more years there has been a slow but steady change in the way people deal with their health issues.

While most Cutting-Edge Boomers were not hippies, the anti-establishment and back-to-nature attitude did have an appeal among many in this age group. Many experimented with drugs that were recommended by friends and many used social situations as a way to "turn on" and "tune out" from the stresses of life. Others believed that processed foods were dangerous and others just wanted to return to a simpler, easier time. So they started to eat healthier. With time, this change began to merge with the notion of eating better and finding natural ways of augmenting food in order to survive in a stressful world. For a growing number of consumers, vitamins and supplements are a part of their regular health routine.

Early on, word-of-mouth and some specialized books and magazines carried the message about natural herbs and supplements. Back then, people primarily purchased the products through a friend, a health food store or, in some instances, via the mail. It was not a big business. Then, as if it were planned, three different types of businesses became inter-related in a way that changed many industries, including what is today's natural food business. The convergence of seemingly unrelated advancements became the foundation of the direct-response industry as we know it today. These three business developments are listed below.

- The expansion of credit card usage fueled people into becoming consumers.

- The establishment of toll-free telephone number services made it easy to call in and order.

- The advent of cable television, which provided more viewer options, created a demand for more programming and offered a lot of cheap airtime. When cable was coupled with the remote control, viewers were able to quickly move through many channels in search of desirable shows.

The Birth of the Infomercial

The above developments led to 30-minute paid programming, which we now call the infomercial. It's funny how the technology of credit cards, toll-free phone service and cable TV took us back to the old days of the snake-oil salesmen. In both instances we were mesmerized by the pitch, we stepped up when asked to participate, and we paid our money hoping that what we bought would deliver the pleasure that was promised. The only difference was that it wasn't two bits (25 cents), it was $29.99, which evolved to a number of payments at $29.99 or more. The viewing public bought everything from vitamins and supplements, to beauty products to exercise equipment. If it could make you look better, feel better or get richer, there were customers ready to buy. It was a great way to buy what you wanted, even if you weren't sure you needed it. Twenty years later, the Direct Response business on TV is still thriving in both the long-form infomercial and the short-form spot versions.

The power of the tube eventually caused viewers to believe that they needed to have these products. Many did not want to order merchandise over the phone, which is the same problem that exists when using a credit card over the Internet today. As a result, consumers were going to their local retailer and requesting what they had seen in a TV infomercial the night before. Our agency's experience with clients that use Direct Response to support their retail stores is that they benefit greatly from the DR effort with very little cannibalization resulting from the dual marketing approach.

The viewers are educated by these commercial shows. Once the consumer becomes involved, they may feel comfortable enough to pick up the phone and place an order. The 30-minute infomercial (it's usually 28 minutes and 30 seconds long) utilizes the AIDA principle to perfection. Attention, interest, desire, and action are the guiding principals in all sales pitches, long or short. The interesting make up about the long-form infomercial is that it's actually several mini-shows woven together by a common product and interrupted by several ordering opportunities. This accomplishes several things. Viewers, armed with their remotes, might drop in on the show at anytime during the half-hour, so they must be able to get up to speed quickly. Those who start at the beginning and don't order early in the show must be retained as a viewer and given additional reasons to buy as the story unfolds. And finally, those who did buy may continue to watch and have their purchase decision validated.

Selling directly to the consumer is not just for late-night hawkers of products that are not readily available in stores. The DR model has become a popular way for many companies to conduct business today. It has also become an effective and efficient way for big ticket items to generate qualified leads. As outbound telemarketing becomes less viable, this response mechanism will be the means of opening more doors. I suspect that this is because some marketers have gained an understanding of the Cutting-Edge Boomer's need for control and how the purchase decision is made.

Earlier, I talked about how there was a line drawn that separated OTC products from ethical drugs. That line was advertising and in the last couple of years that line has been all but obliterated. The pharmaceutical firms are going directly to the patients with television commercials (usually short-form spots), which are backed up by print ads. The commercials promote the benefits while the ads carry all the disclaimers and other legalese.

Some of the most popular problems addressed by these TV solutions are allergies, arthritis, stomach acid, and high cholesterol. However, one that came out of the blue was erectile dysfunction (E.D.). The people who make the product Viagra, the leading prescription to control E.D., are pretty smart. They chose a person to speak for them who was a trusted national figure: former Senator and Republican Presidential candidate Bob Dole. A Purple Heart recipient and war hero, he is a man who has overcome adversities and one who represented the Boomers' parents' generation. It had been publicized that Dole had E.D. as a result of overcoming prostate cancer. He appeared in a TV commercial and admitted the problem and thanked Viagra for making his life normal again. Men of all ages who had this disorder now had hope, and they rushed to their doctors in droves. Sales of Viagra soared as the word got around about this new miracle drug. Even those who didn't have a problem were curious about the drug's effect. More and more men related their symptoms to their doctors, and many of these men literally demanded doctors to write prescriptions.

The Dole spot didn't need to be on the scene too long. It was followed by other spots showing younger men of different ethnicity in staged romantic situations. Now the Viagra spots use Cutting-Edge Boomers, again of various ethnicities, acting like they're newlyweds. One could get the impression that this pill overcomes the daily stress so well that men will not only want to have sex everyday but they'll be able to do it whenever they please. Next thing you know the consumer will be able to buy the product without a prescription, and it will be displayed in the drug store right next to the prophylactics and other contraceptives. Several pharmaceutical firms now market products for E.D., and many natural herbal versions have been introduced and appear to be doing quite well in stores as well as on a Direct Response basis.

We've come full circle with the patients diagnosing their own symptoms and requesting the drug for treatment. The doctors are responding in a positive manner, often prescribing what the patient wants. Why has this phenomenon occurred? Thanks, in a great part, to our healthcare system and, you guessed it, the Boomers. It's the Boomers who sought and found alternative medicines. It's the Boomers who helped push changes in healthcare, which resulted in HMOs and PPOs. This has resulted in a growing number of doctors who don't know their patients, and they can't afford to spend much time with each patient because they now answer to accountants and must follow insurance protocol.

Do these factors sound familiar? Is your business product-oriented, distribution-minded or consumer-focused? Does your business model satisfy the needs and wants of the Cutting-Edge Boomers? Learn everything you can about direct marketing techniques, including those that work and those that failed. Try to spot the emerging trends from other categories and in totally different industries. You can develop incremental business through DR efforts, selling directly to the consumer could fund your ad program, which supports your retail sales. Build your database and start building a relationship with customers. Let your trade accounts know that you are familiar with their customers' needs and wants and that you are communicating with them on a regular basis. This puts you in control of the marketing situation.

The 50+ consumer is a good place to begin testing the DR strategies because this group is in transition. Their media habits and purchasing considerations are changing. Competitors may not be addressing the Cutting-Edge Boomer yet, and success in this segment can be determined quickly then applied to other areas of your business.

Chapter 14

The Growth of Health Consciousness

Good health is a growing concern for the Cutting-Edge Boomer. By now they've seen the physical problems caused by aging as their parents grew older or passed on and friends their age have fallen ill or maybe died suddenly. These reality checks, coupled with the continuing media onslaught about the aging of Americans and advertisers reminding everyone they can look and feel better by using their specific product, keep health issues on the minds of most people, particularly those 50+.

Obviously, good health applies to more than just the physical well being of the individual, it encompasses the emotional and spiritual condition of the person, too. These three factors combine to represent the complete wellness profile of the individual.

Feeling Good and Looking Good

The place where most people begin when discussing their health is the physical aspect. Probably because it's the most apparent and the easiest dimension with which to get in touch with one's self. According to a recent research study conducted for *Newsweek* (2001), an overwhelming number of those 50+ describe their health as good to excellent (80%) and a slightly higher percentage (82%) are satisfied with their physical appearance. Over half of them claim to exercise three times a week or more, with walking representing the mode of exercise participated in by most of those surveyed. However, twice the number of respondents said they exercise less than they did 10 to 20 years ago compared to the number who exercise more. Nearly half said they find it difficult to fit an exercise program into their busy lifestyle.

Eating better is another contributor to good health. When combined with an exercise program, it has a positive effect on reducing heart disease, high blood pressure and cholesterol, diabetes, obesity, and more. However, about a third of the respondents in the *Newsweek* study said they weren't eating enough fruits and vegetables and weren't limiting their intake of red meats and fatty foods, while nearly 40% had problems reducing the amount of sugar they ate. This suggests that there seems to be a distinction between what's smart to eat and what's savory. With the instant gratification, the "Me" generation knows what's smart but usually settles for what is savory.

It's why the 50+ Boomers jumped on the fat-free bandwagon. Whether they were health conscious or not, consumers saw this as an easy way to lose weight. Unfortunately, too much of a good thing for those not committed to a watchful diet and exercise resulted in many Americans becoming more obese. The premise was that eating fat-free foods meant automatically losing weight; therefore one could eat as much as they wanted and still lose weight. The problem was that people ate too much of the prepared fat-free entrees. Eating a whole box of fat-free cookies after dinner and three scoops of fat-free yogurt destroyed the weight loss programs for these so-called dieters.

Being a generation of extremes, the 50+ Boomers heard what they wanted to hear. Fat-free was interchangeable with calorie free. Of course, those who gained weight using the fat-free approach later came to the realization that most fat-free products contained more calories than the regular or higher fat version of the product. Otherwise, these foods would fall short on the savory scale. This just confirms the old adage "there's no such thing as a free lunch." The Cutting-Edge Boomers who were already on some kind of health-oriented program did not seem to have these problems, but those who thought they could eat their way to weight loss had a rude awakening.

It's strange that faster lifestyles and greater overall stress have not spurred an increase in exercise activities for the 50+ Boomers. In fact, these consumers tend to be more prone to obesity than previous generations. Today's busy lives are more involved with non-physical activities. However, as the Cutting-Edge Boomers continue to age, their doctors may become important influences in the way this group eats and exercises. This could have a profound effect on the future of preventative medicine.

A healthy populace is more productive and reduces direct and indirect costs for business, government and the individuals. So the longer people stay well, the better it is for everyone. You can expect insurance companies to offer more favorable rates to people who pursue and stick to exercise programs. These programs will be prescribed and monitored by their doctors under codes approved by the policy provider. This isn't farfetched. People who don't smoke get lower rates, so why isn't it a logical progression to reward those who are taking positive actions to improve their health. As this idea catches on, maintaining an exercise routine to reduce certain health problems, which can be improved through regular physical activity, will earn discounted rates for the policy holder as certain plateaus are reached.

Imagine improving your health and actually saving money as a result.

Of course, a body that operates better is only part of the benefit derived from exercise. Stress reduction is another important aspect that many people overlook. With the Cutting-Edge Boomers being in their peak earning years, they undoubtedly are experiencing their peak stress years. All exercise has a positive effect on one's mental condition because focusing on the task at hand diverts attention from the causes of stress. This delivers a synergistic health benefit to the person involved in the activity. Again, this is something the insurance firms must consider one of these days.

Completing the trilogy, so to speak, is the spiritual aspect of wellness. Meditation helps release the cares of the world, as does participating in one's chosen religion. However, disciplines such as yoga encompass all three areas of health: body, mind and spirit. The 50+ Boomers in their youth were exposed to alternative means of dealing with these issues, from Eastern religions to mind-altering drugs; however, the exercise part of the equation wasn't too high on their lists back then. Recognizing a need, these Cutting-Edge Boomers should be open to a variety of methods designed to attain their wellness goals. Businesses that can provide these services have a bright future.

A Fountain of Youth and Opportunity

As people become more aware of themselves, they will also better appreciate what goes into their bodies. Nutritional education is an ongoing process. The Cutting-Edge Boomers have had a half-century of learning about the subject. Now they're faced with doing something about what they eat or they may possibly pay the price in the not too distant future. Even if they don't have an immediate problem, parents or friends might.

This translates to a growing business for vitamins and supplements, as consumers learn about free radicals, antioxidants and a whole host of other factors which could affect their health. Issues like genetically altered produce and grains have become concerns that must be addressed on packaged food labels. Green teas and other herbal and holistic products are getting attention as well. Once considered specialty products, tofu and soy-based foods are enjoying widespread growth, especially the latter since taste and textures of these products have been significantly improved.

Where will the 50+ Boomers look for these products? Not in the health food stores! Sure there's a small segment of the population that shops in natural and nutritional retail outlets, but the busy Boomer doesn't have the time nor the inclination to patronize these stores in addition to the traditional ones they frequent already. Besides, many of these consumers feel uncomfortable in these stores. They don't know where to find things, are overwhelmed by the unfamiliar surroundings and unknown brands, and asking might prove to be embarrassing. So their favorite supermarket or drug store better stock these health products or it might not be their favorite store anymore. The future for buying many of these products through Direct Response marketing efforts is a likely possibility in the short term. However, as more people use them, products not currently in general retail distribution will be available through mainstream stores.

Healthier Vacation Options

As an increasing number of 50+ Boomers are taking better care of themselves, vacations designed to complement their improved lifestyles will take on greater importance. Instead of rushing their way through Europe doing seven cities in seven days, less hectic but possibly more physical itineraries could gain interest. These would require, for example, more walking and incorporate more excursions into the countryside. Mediterranean beach properties with organized activities throughout the day and spa menus could attract many health-conscious Americans.

In this country, affordable spas at the beach or in the mountains will continue to bring exercise, diet and the spiritual elements together. This will allow the stressed-out Cutting-Edge Boomer to take a vacation and truly recharge their batteries. Nothing can be better than returning from vacation and not feeling the need for another vacation or the pressure to shed pounds due to overindulging while away. There are currently some such hideaways around the country. However, many of them have either a communal atmosphere with nuts and twigs featured on the menus or are for the well to do with a lot of pampering and little exercise, topped off with really good food but really small portions.

It seems to me that a couple of the big hospitality chains could offer this total physical, relaxation and smart-eating package as an option at a few of their existing resorts much like the cruise lines do. Of course, a forward-thinking independent operator could take what they already offer and tweak the concept a bit to make it the perfect vacation alternative for the 50+ Boomer. It's a concept whose time has come.

Think about the ramifications of exercise, stress reduction, meditation and spirituality combined with better eating, which also satisfies the need for more energy and the overall preservation of good health. Whether it's consumables (products or services) used as a part of the 50+ Boomers' daily activities or the change-of-pace offerings that are part of a vacation, health marketing provides real growth potential.

Chapter 15

Other Businesses Can Benefit from a Boomer-Friendly Approach

Supermarket and drug store products are not the only areas where an understanding of the Cutting-Edge Boomers can be translated into extra sales and profits for you.

Most Mall Stores Do Not Stand Out

The modern mall offers many opportunities for marketing to women and, to a lesser extent, men. However, a brief tour of such operations may indicate that these facilities are not particularly Cutting-Edge Boomer friendly. Many clothing boutiques and shoe stores cater to those in their teens and early twenties. In fact, many parents take their teenage daughters with them when they shop, but separate once there. Many teenagers get dropped off at the mall for the movies or just to do their own thing. So malls have become hang outs for kids as well as a place where they can spend all of their available cash. Because these young people haven't acquired any debt yet, their money can all be spent on impulse purchases.

Women who are above the age of 50 account for nearly 40% of all apparel sales (U.S. Bureau of the Census, 1997). So why are the mall stores ignoring this valuable consumer, with the possible exception of the anchor department stores and a few specialty shops? Even the department stores have reduced or eliminated home furnishings and other traditional offerings in favor of expanding the fad clothing sections. Does this suggest that a "Boomer's Boutique" might be a viable addition to the mall line-up? The boutique would not play heart pounding, head thumping music; sales people would be adults (this requires higher-paid professionals), who would act and dress like adults; and the selection of clothes would be above a size two. The boutiques could carry quality merchandise and stock classic styles, not just the latest fads. Other offerings could be cosmetics with a more mature woman in mind, a premium gift section, concierge service, and other products and services that could make this type of store an attractive alternative to what is now being presented. Nordstrom's Department Store offers such things but an individual smaller store should see merit in this concept. Perhaps a manufacturer in this field could package such a program and become the primary supplier in this category.

For most men, a trip to the mall is a fate worse than death. If we must go maybe there's a Hammacher Schlemmer, Sharper Image or Brookstone store to amuse us. Otherwise, there's little to interest the average guy, especially the Cutting-Edge Boomer. Perhaps a Boomer Boutique could have something for men too, such as a place to sit and read, or watch TV, or computers with online access. This could be a store that could help men with purchasing gifts for their loved ones. Many Boomer men and women would walk past scores of other stores to get to one that was dedicated to serving their needs. And unlike the other stores, this one wouldn't have to be promoting a sale every week to attract customers.

What Do Discount Stores Offer the 50+ Boomer?

An area where you can expect to see a decline in Cutting-Edge Boomer traffic is the discount, variety, and mass merchant stores. Just as the club and warehouse stores appeal to budget-minded families, so do these discounters. Empty-Nesters will pay a little more for the convenience and less hectic pace that service stores provide. Appliances, TVs, computers and other electronic gear, are possible exceptions that could bring the Boomers into these discounters because these are larger ticket items, which are purchased less frequently. For the rest of the merchandise, the 50+ Boomer would rather go elsewhere, so this class of retailer ought to look at ways to appeal to what could eventually become a vanishing customer. Other things like service departments where a sale could be rung up allowing the customer to bypass the long check out lines, or creating a grandparent's department may make these discounters more Boomer friendly. Hardware and garden centers that function as stores within the store and have trained employees are already featured at many outlets. Hobby and specialty units might be placed around the perimeter of the core building to create the impression of being part of the store while providing individual service. If these chains were to offer such amenities, they must promote it through the right media and deliver on their promises; otherwise, a poor execution of a 50+ Boomer's concept will drive consumers away and keep them away. Done well, the smart merchandiser will have opened the door to a long-term relationship with these focused consumers.

These considerations, which may have already been investigated and tested by some retailers somewhere, may not directly apply to your business. However, these ideas should stimulate your creative process and cause you to think about the 50+ Boomer in new ways, opening up new avenues of providing this consumer with the right products and services. This should help you build a better relationship with this important emerging consumer. Let's look at a few more categories and a few more concepts to stimulate your thinking.

'Have It Your Way' Should Be More Than a Slogan

Restaurant operators certainly want to attract the free spending 50+ consumer. In a consumer expenditure survey projected to the year 2000, the U.S. Bureau of Labor Statistics (1995) found that Boomers account for nearly 40% of all restaurant meals eaten in this country. They're more likely to order a drink or wine than dessert, and their check averages, as well as tips, are higher. But early bird specials aren't going to entice this crowd. In fact, mostly everything about that kind of promotion is unappetizing to Cutting-Edge Boomers: They're too busy to get to the restaurant early and they like food with a little more pizzazz.

So what's going to get the 50+ Boomer through the door and encourage them to come back? Restaurateurs should take a tip from our earlier discussion about supermarkets and offer healthier meals. But they must be sure that the food tastes good— flavorful and not too spicy. As stated earlier, even those who are health conscious aren't willing to order something at a restaurant that they could easily prepare at home; however, some comfort foods such as meatloaf are exceptions to that rule. Many people like to see the "heart-healthy" symbol as reassurance that the restaurant serves healthy food. Lean and tender meats, a variety of fresh seafood, and chicken prepared in more than one way appeals to everyone. Sensible portions may also be of greater concern to many of the 50+ Boomers.

The issue of greatest importance is service. As stated earlier, Boomers will pay for it and still consider the meal a value. Service begins at the front door and continues until the customer leaves. Service is attitude, being around to take care of things, anticipating needs and handling wants; it's being the customer's advocate, and making the dining experience as pleasant as possible. Although this sounds simple, many of the service personnel fall short on one or more of these measurement dimensions. Often, everything's fine until the customer has a problem or complaint, and that's when a breakdown occurs. Suddenly, the server and even the manager take a defensive position and the relationship becomes adversarial.

This happens all too often in all too many businesses. If you don't subscribe to "the customer is always right" philosophy, you will always lose. Customers who leave with unresolved problems or a feeling of being mistreated will not be return customers. This is especially true when dealing with the "Me" generation. The restaurants that train their employees to provide continuous and courteous service will give their patrons many reasons to keep coming back, and the servers will probably notice the customer satisfaction in the tips they receive.

The 50+ Boomers Have Different Reasons for Buying a Car

Automobiles will continue to be bought by the Cutting-Edge Boomers for many years to come. Most of them will buy or lease several cars in the next 20 or more years. This means that it's not too late to develop a relationship with this potential repeat purchaser. However, it must be understood that the Boomer's needs and wants are likely to shift dramatically in the next few years. Now they're experiencing the peak earning potential and are not too concerned about the future. This is the time to sell them a new car, probably with the extra comfort and safety accessories. Whether you're an auto manufacturer, an individual dealer, an association, or an ad agency, you will have to stay close to this customer and track their thinking as they progress into their 60s and on to retirement. That way, you'll know who to direct the advertising to and what appeals will make them respond. Downsizing, or a previously owned car, might be a later option. The best way to obtain this information is through one-on-one research conducted by the service departments of dealerships, in conjunction with phone and mail surveys done under the auspices of the factory.

More and more 50+ Boomers are using the Internet to compare features and prices. Don't ignore the opportunity of using your website as a way to let this specific audience know what you can do for them. No one ever wants to be sold a car by the kind of pressure selling that this industry is known for. Emphasizing service, before and after the sales transaction, is the only way to keep the 50+ Boomer happy.

The 50+ Boomer Is Still a Factor in the Real Estate Market

The last big purchase the Cutting-Edge Boomer might make is the purchase of a home. Once they become Empty-Nesters, what they're living in could be too large for their needs. Because they are going to be working for another 10 or 20 years, these Boomers will probably want to stay close to where they currently live. They will want less grass to cut and undoubtedly less overall up-keep and operating expense. A condo could be of interest, but too many stairs to climb could be a problem later. Some won't mind doing a little fixing up and remodeling since they'll probably have some extra money resulting from the sale of a larger home and buying a smaller home. This could also be true for renters simply wanting to downsize as well.

There are many businesses that could benefit from being in the loop on any real estate transaction involving the 50+ Boomer. Of course, the Realtor who lists the first home and helps find the second is really in a profitable position. This is not an unusual situation because it's normally a local move. Interior designers, home-furnishing stores, remodeling firms even hardware stores and garden centers in the area of the new home can gain business. Although it may only be a one-family move, businesses that network with the Realtor as the lynchpin can pay off for all that are involved. The key is to know when the move is about to occur and mount a marketing effort directed toward the family that is relocating. Personal contact and direct mail can be most effective even though this is the most basic of grass roots efforts, it works.

The Cutting-Edge Boomers and those who follow have demonstrated a propensity to spend, even through questionable economic times. There is no evidence that their desire to purchase goods and services that improve or sustain their quality of life will be tempered in the near future. Even those who have not realized financial success in their lives will continue to seek the material things even if they have to stretch to do it.

The 50+ consumer has many needs and wants that have not been met so they are in a transitional state. This means that the Cutting-Edge Boomers may not be expressing, or even realizing, what they expect from you. You must do the research for them, test the concepts that you believe have merit and refine them to perfection. The time and money that you invest in building a business with the 50+ Boomers will pay off for years to come.

Chapter 16

Service Still Means Something

As discussed in the last few chapters, service is a vital part of the evaluation process and in making the decision to buy. This applies to mostly all products, from packaged goods to durables to big-ticket items. This is also a key factor in the determination of where to buy these products. Now, let's look at service as it applies to what constitutes the vast segment commonly known as the "service industry."

For simplicity sake, "service" will be defined as "any sale that does not include a tangible product as part of the transaction, yet requires an immediate or long range commitment to perform some function by the seller on behalf of the purchaser." This obviously covers a wide field. So let's begin by taking a look at what might come to the minds of the 50+ Boomers if asked to list important service categories.

Financial Institutions Should Seek Out the 50+ Boomer

The most important service would likely be financial services. This vast industry, made up of many segments, has undergone more changes than most of the product-oriented areas. Banking, for instance, was a solid but staid business for over 50 years following the stock market crash in 1929 and the Depression that ensued. During that period, there were commercial banks, savings and loans, savings banks, and later credit unions.

Commercial banks had the most services to offer. Although the others were restricted from offering the full range of services that banks did; they paid higher interest rates on savings accounts. Some 20 years ago, the restrictions were lifted apparently making the playing field level. However, deregulation actually made the players too similar. Now there was no reason to have money in one place for checking and another for savings and so on. It had become a commodity business again and, in light of the new marketing conditions, a firm's personality now needed to be re-evaluated.

Financial institutions found themselves in the same situation as the grocery retailers. The banks had more plans or services to offer consumers while supermarkets had more products. Both were in the commodity business, with price being a tangible factor and quality as well as service not being distinctively different from the competition. Those with a discernable service differentiation tended to be smaller operations with limited marketing resources. So the larger operators came to the conclusion that the best way to compete was to get bigger. Banks bought other banks; savings and loan associations bought other savings and loan associations. Everybody became a bank of sorts, with the exception of the credit unions, which operated within the companies or unions with which they had their charters. By achieving critical mass, the new financial entities hoped to gain the consumer's business by virtue of being convenient. After buying or driving out the smaller chains and independents, the few remaining banking chains had branches in most communities making them the neighborhood bank, much in the way the big supermarket chains became dominant in the local food business.

To assimilate more locations, the operations departments became the primary force within the organizations. Marketing went about trying to build the bank's image and the promise of higher rates on savings and lower rates on loans was the real difference between the banks. Because they all alluded to better service and quality, significant differences did not really exist. Awareness was the key objective of the marketing efforts and many branches knew that money spent on advertising would yield a greater share of market.

However, service seems to have suffered along the way. The notion of having a personal banker vanished. Fewer tellers were working inside, convenient drive-through windows further reduced contact with customers, and automated-teller machines coupled with automatic payroll deposit and now banking over the Internet has forced us to put our trust in machines rather than people. But in the age of dehumanization in this industry, some institutions have managed to create a feeling of trust. Most notable in the western part of the country is Wells Fargo Bank. They still use the stagecoach and the concept of "we deliver" based on over a hundred years of keeping their promise. This bigger-than-life campaign has been running, with some variations for longer than most people on the West Coast can remember. In fact, the Cutting-Edge Boomers grew up with it. Maybe that's why Wells Fargo is such a dominant factor in its mature markets today.

The Boomers Know Better

Cutting-Edge Boomers remember when there were full-service banks, meaning these institutions offered to provide all banking needs under one roof. They also can recall when full-service brokerage firms were the only ones that consumers trusted for stocks and bond transactions. Boomers can point to the time when full-service insurance companies offered all kinds of protection against loss—life, limbs, house, and car. Today, the distinctions between the various plans offered by these kinds of companies have become rather fuzzy for the Cutting-Edge Boomer. This consumer understood the differences until they reached their 30s. Now that they're in their 50s, they are not sure who to call about which financial services or why.

There's a demand for personalized service again. The 50+ Boomers are individualistic and want to be recognized as such. Being a number doesn't appeal to them. Boomers are going to become more cautious with their investment strategies if they haven't done so already. They have money in banks with many more dollars in individual retirement accounts (IRAs), stocks, bonds, mutual funds, certificates of deposit (CDs) and more. If an Empty-Nester sells a house and downsizes, what's going to happen to the profits? The government doesn't tax a gain from a sale of up to $250,000 once a person reaches 55, so finding a place for the money in your bank can land a customer who remains a customer for years to come. Banks should be getting some of this long-term money invested in the products they offer.

Partnering programs can be developed for banks to market various services in conjunction with others who want to reach the same Cutting-Edge consumer. But unless the banks get into the business of servicing people, they will be seeing less and less money. Stockbrokers, insurance companies, and financial planners of all descriptions are all vying for the 50+ Boomer's money and positioning themselves to handle the rest of the Boomers. As previously stated, successful businesses will build a relationship with the consumer through "trust marketing." This will require everyone in the organization to understand the needs and provide the kind of service wanted by this powerful consumer group. The customers should have access to an organization's people, quickly and easily. They need to have a feeling of satisfaction when the transaction is completed. Whether it's by phone, fax, letter, email, or better yet face-to-face, nothing beats a friendly, competent and swift resolution to a problem or question. Are you willing to do whatever it takes to instill this kind of thinking and discipline in all your employees? If so, you will surely be known as a service oriented company.

Banks could get a bigger piece of the investment pie if they just made it easier to do business with them. These institutions have sophisticated computer systems, so why not establish one general account for the consumers and help them with their personal budgeting while offering various ways to earn greater interest? The customer decides what they want to save for, and they also determine how much may be needed and over what period of time and how it will be used. Personal counselors and the website can help with these decisions. They can add new saving categories as needed, and once the goal is reached, additional savings suggestions could be made. Each individual account can be included as a line item in the general account, and they should earn interest on the combined line items. This would also include an interest-earning checking account. As the total grows, the account could move up in interest earned and long-term savings could be rolled over into CDs and other higher earning options to generate a greater return. This simple concept differentiates the banks' services, adds the personal touch and keeps more of the consumer's dollars in one place. There are many other ways to bundle services, but don't rely on rack brochures and statement stuffers to tell the story. Instead make what you offer important to them by designing something that's personalized for the 50+ customers.

When maximizing a savings account and investing money as wisely as possible, it would make sense to have the soundest advice. Yet many Boomers are not getting it and don't know where to go to get it. You'll recall that this is the anti-establishment generation that did not trust American institutions. Now many Boomers are in a rather unfavorable financial planning predicament and probably don't even realize how this happened. You need to become their friend, without being selfserving and show them how you can help.

Sometimes it's rather difficult to determine what motivates these consumers financial thought processes. They were willing, after the Iranian hostage situation and oil shortage was resolved, to keep pumping their own gas because it was no big deal. They were younger then and this was a way of saving some money and being independent. Yet, when asked to bag their own groceries to save a few cents, they refused. They were willing to go to discount brokers to trade their stocks and bonds thus bypassing research and other personal services because the other guys charged too much and didn't seem to know all that much anyway. This attitude helped get the Boomer investors into tech stocks because it was an emerging trend, and they always had a friend with the inside information on what to buy. So they saved money and had some great growth stocks in their portfolios.

Then came the dot com phenomenon and with that the online trading companies, and investing changed from a business to a game. Day trading was like going to the crap tables at Vegas; the only difference is that you know you're gambling when you go to the casinos. When trouble hit, people got out of the dot com stocks but many kept using the online trading systems. Is this because they trust their own decision-making process more than those of a stock broker? Perhaps it's arrogance or fear that motivates these kinds of decisions. As a result of the Enron scandal, the 50+ investor may look for future help from those with impeccable credentials in an effort to preserve and increase their savings as the earning years become fewer. As the Cutting-Edge Boomers come to the crossroads of the financial planning aspects of their lives, they must get in touch with the emotions that drive them to make choices and the marketers must be in tune with how to deal with them as well.

What Will the Future Hold?

After turning 50, life is marked by a series of events that have important financial implications. Becoming Empty-Nesters, having grandchildren, buying a smaller home, retiring, moving into a senior facility and other such events through the later years of life offer significant opportunities for the insurance and stock people to provide service packages. Companies could offer insurance that changes with the phases of life. Taking disability insurance and converting it to supplement health insurance and/or extended care insurance will hold on to a customer by not forcing them to re-qualify at each stage of life for each new type of insurance. It stands to reason that a life policy is more likely to be placed with a company who is trusted to handle the rest of the long-range insurance plans. This same type of thinking should apply to the stock and other investment markets. Not just lip service, but real personalized planning for moving monies from one form of investment to another. If you are in this business, consider reducing the commissions since you'll be earning them over a longer period of time as those customers move from growth stocks to earnings stocks and mutual funds to whatever is right for them at each phase. All along, you'll be helping them reach their personal goals. Yes, it's supposed to be that way now, but is it really? In early 2002, I noticed that Allstate Insurance was using the Beatles' song *When I'm 64* in a TV commercial to promote its full range of insurance services. This advertising was obviously aimed at the 50+ consumer, but I do not know if the coverage offered was also tailored to this audience—the commercial certainly was.

A lack of trust, not wanting to be hurt, fear of intimacy and a growing list of character defects and emotional hang-ups have definite marketing implications. How can the 50+ Boomer really believe what the big insurance companies say about the need for long-term care insurance? If they listen to the brokerage firms they could continue to take a beating in the stock market. Getting too close to a financial advisor results in too much personal information being disclosed. However, to adequately prepare for the future, these Boomers have to get over this kind of thinking. Marketers must build trust through understanding the potential problem, with general information about possible solutions, and later through a one-on-one type of relationship that helps the individual make the decision that's right for them through the guidance of a personal advisor.

Notice I said one-on-one, not face-to-face, when referring to a personal relationship with the consumer. That's because a great deal of the work can be done through mail, fax, phone and email. Routine forms and simple follow up can be efficiently handled via these alternative methods This does not suggest that these are the preferred methods, just some of the alternatives. Nothing will replace the effectiveness that comes as a result of being face-to-face with a customer or prospect. However, it's up to you to decide when to sit across from the customer and help them reach a decision that will make them feel good about doing business with you long after they have signed on the dotted line.

Dealing with the 50+ Boomer's financial security is a sacred trust that cannot become a reality overnight. Patience coupled with appropriate persistence is the tried and true approach to earning this consumer's respect; this is the essence of "Trust Marketing." The company and individual who realizes that establishing trust, building the relationship and providing individual-ized service for the Cutting-Edge Boomer will be the ones to reap the benefits of what they sow today for many years to come.

Chapter 17

The Sandwich Generation

The 50+ Boomers are truly a sandwiched generation. In addition to planning for their own future, many of them have living parents who require care, plus they may be caring for children who are not totally self supporting. There was a time when people looked forward to the prospects of retirement. Sitting on the porch with the morning coffee and the newspaper then doing whatever one pleased throughout the rest of the day was a romantic dream of what the golden years would be like. It probably was a concept that was created by past generations from years of hard work, and it kept people going as they edged closer to the age of 65. For much of the past century, the typical retiree only lived a couple of years past retirement age. Most men didn't last too long beyond retirement and their spouses normally outlived them. The spouse ended up living alone on the benefits left behind or moved in with a family member. Such was life for most of the past century.

Today, the situation is very different. Chances are that both parents of the Cutting-Edge Boomers are still alive. Most of them are living in their own homes, many in the house in which the children were raised, while others live in an apartment or retirement community. And, being both proud and independent, they'll be on their own as long as the two of them are alive. As the years pass by, the Cutting-Edge Boomer will quickly become a more important part of the care-giving equation.

The 50+ Boomers Have Many Concerns about Healthcare

With modern medical breakthroughs, it won't be uncommon in the future for 50+ Boomers, who have reached retirement age, to have either or both parents living. That means some of the group may have as few as 10 years to prepare for the financial trauma that could be waiting for them. Here's why I believe this coming event could be devastating. Parents of the Boomers were more savings oriented and many worked for companies that had retirement plans, which were the rage back in the 1960s and 1970s. However, these parents have a good chance of outliving their savings. Additionally, long-term care insurance was not available back then, and healthcare costs have gone through the roof. Even though the aging Boomers won't completely retire at the age of 65 or even 70, their peak earning years will be behind them, leaving them saddled with the possibility of having to support their parents as well as themselves.

The 1999 AARP/ Roper Starch Report shows that most of the 50+ Boomers—more than two-thirds of them—have not adequately prepared financially for their own retirement years. As a result, 8 out of 10 of them expect to work after they retire. Not only are they seriously underfunded for living on a fixed income, most haven't purchased long-term care insurance or made the arrangements for future healthcare contingencies. This young-thinking "I can always make more money" crowd is in for a rude awakening if they make the transition from being the "sandwich generation" to that of the "caught in a vise generation." They don't want to hear about not being ready for what may lie ahead, but they certainly need help with understanding, planning and implementing programs that can contribute to a more secure future.

The Cutting-Edge Boomers did not start reaching 55 until 2001 and the economy was still robust through 2000. There was little interest in, and less thought given to, the notion of caregiving. Even now, unless there's an absolutely identifiable need, both the aging parents and their aging children don't want to discuss it. While it's too late in the game to purchase long-term care insurance for parents, it may well be the best time for the 50+ Boomers to qualify and buy it. That way a 10-pay plan can be paid for by the time they reach 65, or a continuing pay program can be obtained at a lower premium. If you're in the insurance business, this is a potentially red-hot marketing opportunity.

Consider packaging a limited-coverage plan for the parents and the extended plan for the Boomer children. It would give both generations security and provide you, as the marketer, with an entry point for providing more of the family's insurance coverage. The only problem I see is that most carriers haven't had sufficient experience in offering this type of care insurance, so they're not well equipped to develop custom plans that would effectively meet individual needs. However, this situation is going to change quickly.

There are a number of services that caregivers are going to require to allow them to properly provide for their parents. According to a National Alliance for Caregiving survey (1996), over 80 percent of those being cared for are mothers or mothers-in-law, and the ones performing the care are mostly women who work outside the home. Some 80 percent of the caregivers don't live with those they care for; the majority live within a 20 minute commute.

Nearly 20 hours of care is required each week on the part of the caregiver. Services provided are transportation, grocery and other shopping, meal preparation, cleaning and finance management. In addition, the care recipient may require assistance with personal activities and this is a major burden on the life of the caregiver. Because they want to provide care as well as support to the loved one, most women in the 50+ group will try to do everything themselves and often the stress is too much.

According to *Modern Maturity* (September 2001), ethnicity plays a major role in who provides service. The publication stated that 42 percent of Asian Americans were caregivers to their parents. The numbers fell to 34 percent for Hispanics, 28 percent for African Americans and 19 percent for whites. Those born outside the United States are far more likely to provide care or support (43 percent) versus those who are U.S. born (20 percent). The numbers change dramatically for the sandwich generation, approximately 70 percent don't want to have their children care for them in their old age.

The higher percentages of family caring by foreign-born children may be due in part to lower income, not just cultural traditions of providing care for the aging. Nonetheless, older family members continue to need care. Service organizations offering dependable help will grow in demand. As more extended care insurance is sold, more levels of care will be covered, especially services that combine household care with personal care. A workforce of unskilled laborers, as well as first-generation immigrants, will perform such activities. In addition, retired citizens, who want to supplement their incomes while helping others, could return to the part-time workforce. In many instances, caregiving might utilize the talents of both groups of workers.

Until the care receiver chooses to move into a senior housing facility or is forced to do so based on their health, outside service providers can augment or almost totally take over the caregiver activities as long as those doing the hiring have the ability to pay. Once the aging family member gives up their home or apartment, the final passage can be rather expensive. If the aging parent of the Boomer does not move into their offspring's home, which has initial upfront costs and long-term psychological implications, outside living and care service must be considered.

Independent living can range from a single apartment in a senior complex to those that provide full-service including meals, staff nursing, entertainment, cleaning and everything else needed for complete care of the individual. Of course, the more one pays the more one receives. People seem to wait as long as they can before moving to such facilities, with the average age of residents being well into their 80s.

Assisted living is the next natural stage. This is a service that can be provided at home or in a senior facility. This includes feeding, dressing, bathing and toileting as well as help with walking and other mobility needs. The final phase, which is skilled nursing, requires qualified medical help most, if not all, of the time. As the family member moves from one level of care to the next, costs increase accordingly.

Any help you can give the Cutting-Edge Boomer today, to prepare them financially and psychologically for tomorrow, can result in an immediate pay off for the forward thinking marketer. Having figured out a way to care for their parents and insure themselves for future healthcare needs doesn't mean the 50+ Boomer can relax. Remember, their parent's are the first segment of the sandwich generation. It wasn't that long ago that their children left, and if things don't go according to plan, they might be back.

The Empty Nest Fills Up Again

In some parts of the country, many of the Boomer's children had high-paying jobs with dot com firms and high tech companies, only to be laid off with the tech-sector crash. Others just could not make it on their own. Some of the Boomers' daughters are single mothers. These factors have led some of these children back home, changing the lives of those Boomers who had thought they were Empty-Nesters.

The re-introduction of a 20-something child into the home isn't going to change their lifestyles much since both the child and the parents will want their independence. While there may be some friction, it won't affect buying habits very much, if at all. More junk food may find its way into the house, and redecorating the guestroom will be put off for a while. However, if a daughter moves back with a baby, some dramatic changes may occur.

Naturally the baby becomes the center of attention. Remodeling the baby's room and maybe the mother's could be in order. Family meals and shopping trips become the rule rather than the exception. The Boomer grandparents become the babysitters as the daughter goes out with friends or on dates in an effort to get her life back together. The grandparents' life is put on hold until the daughter moves on. When this happens, it becomes a mixed blessing. Eventually things return to an Empty-Nester lifestyle again and the regular buying patterns resume.

Being an Empty-Nester Can Be Fun and Profitable

After becoming an Empty-Nester, these people will be changing the way they live as well as the environment in which they live. The 50+ Boomers and their older counterparts represent the highest percentage of homeowners. They view their homes as an investment and the government agrees by allowing them to sell these properties for profits without taxation. Therefore, putting money into upgrading or remodeling now can produce a greater long-term return for the homeowner by increasing the property's value. Additionally, if they decide to stay in their current home, extra disposable income becomes available after the children leave. Because this is the "Me" generation, they still believe that they deserve the beauty and comfort they've worked hard to achieve. Finally, those that downsize should have plenty of money to make their smaller quarters reflect the convenience they need and the style in which they want to live.

Extra rooms will not lie idle. These Cutting-Edge Boomers will transform them into offices, exercise rooms and home theaters. In addition, hobby rooms and workshops will emerge where storage and garage space once existed. The first to benefit from the empty-nest phenomenon could be the real estate people, then the mortgage brokers and others within the financial community, if downsizing sales occur. However, whether they sell or stay put, the positive effect of the Empty-Nester's renewed interest in their homes will be felt by many businesses.

Architects, contractors and designers (interior and exterior) will be the first to benefit from the Boomer's home. Then, the home centers, garden outlets, furniture and appliance stores, and the cabinetmakers will follow as the Boomers remodel and upgrade. Finally, the electronic retailers will sell the latest computer and electronic gadgetry needed to connect these Cutting-Edge Boomers with the outside world.

The sandwich generation has the prospect of taking care of their parents while their children still depend on them for support. Once the 50+ Boomers have tended to these family matters, they will be able to rearrange their living situation for their own convenience and enjoyment. This makes them a big-spending consumer for home-related products and services.

Chapter 18

September 11, 2001: How the Boomers Can Lead Us Out of the Shadows

What happened to the social concerns that the Boomers demonstrated about in the 1960s and 1970s? Man's injustices have not been eliminated, but they have been somewhat rectified and improved. Are yesterday's activists leading the causes of today? No way. People change with time and their priorities change with life's experiences. As family and personal security become more important, the "Me" generation has put its focus on matters closer to home.

The "Me" generation actually has only two major concerns: getting what they want and keeping what they've already got. That's a far cry from the great causes of their bygone youth. However, these self-centered concerns may just be what will reunite the Cutting-Edge Boomers into a solid political block again. They have come together in the recent past to help elect and re-elect Bill Clinton. His "I feel your pain" approach worked particularly well with Boomer women. However, this same group split their vote in the 2000 election, making it a dead heat.

Yet at this stage in their lives, the 50+ Boomers have not found reasons to bond together. Most can see past the differences of race, gender and even sexual preferences to accept the similarities they share with each other. They realize that when it's all said and done, we all have the same needs and wants. However, the various segments that make up this group may not be on common ground when determining how these needs and wants are to be satisfied.

During the 1960s and into the 1970s, many of the Cutting-Edge Boomers had distrust for many of this nation's institutions—social, religious and governmental. They felt that these institutions were to blame for many of the wrongs done to mankind. As legislative changes came, the oppressed became the recipients of more ambitious spending programs and received the benefits of equal opportunity and affirmative action programs. The pendulum began to swing. Suddenly, the government, at least the liberal side of it, became a friend to minorities and women. Those who didn't have a nuclear family, in the traditional sense, had the government to depend on and take care of them. Of course, this left those who were not in these groups in the position of paying for such programs. Many did not like this government interference, so the gap began to widen.

A Decade of Things Being Good

There is an issue that's going to grow bigger and bigger with each passing day for the 50+ Boomer: retirement. This single word takes on the all-encompassing question of "what's going to happen to me for the rest of my life?" Retirement is an event like death, which is years away, yet as inevitable as taxes. The major considerations are when to stop working and how good will quality of life be once the paychecks cease.

The "Me" generation has earned more and enjoys a better quality of life than previous generations, thanks in part to dual-income families. However, they spend more and are deeper in debt than their earlier counterparts were at this same age. A higher lifestyle will also mean more sacrifices for many as their earning capabilities decrease and fixed incomes dictate many of the decisions in their lives. Until recently, I believed the state of the economy in general would be good enough to carry the Cutting-Edge Boomers to their early 60s before really worrying about the "R" word. Wow, things have changed!

A strong stock market, even if showing little short-term growth, would keep 401K accounts solid and consumer confidence on the positive side of the ledger. Even the optimists knew that tech stocks were in for an adjustment after doubling in value in recent years. Employment was expected to dip after a long run as well. Over the Summer of 2001, the NASDAQ continued to tank and the Dow-Jones index dipped below 10,000 in early September 2001. Consumers were getting concerned and the constant chipping away at interest rates by the Federal Reserve Bank along with the tax rebates was not having the hoped for effect.

Then Tragedy Struck

Then came September 11, 2001, the day of the terrorists' attack from the shadows. In four separate but related acts of terrorism, the fragility of our financial strength and the reality of our mortality came crashing down on all Americans and all the people in the world. Fear raised its ugly head and the hopes and dreams of the future drifted away in the smoke that rose from the rubble of the World Trade Center. The renewed patriotism and outpouring of funds for the victims proves how great we are as a people and demonstrates how quickly we can unite.

Now the financial future of everyone, especially the 50+ Boomer, is a big question. If the Wall Street bears, who have been waiting for their opportunities, can convince those on the fence that gloom and doom is the developing picture, the already tenuous market will continue its downward slide. Perhaps when the consumer confidence is based on reality and inflated stock values are adjusted, the bulls will be back in favor again. Nonetheless, the stock portfolios of many Boomers shows their savings at nearly half its worth from the end of 2000. This means they'll be working for the next several years just to be where they were a year or so ago. Many will put their savings into less risky investments, which offer more security but lower returns.

What will the wartime mentality do to business? Will there be higher costs? It looks as if the airlines will have to charge more to offset the costs for greater security. What will happen to the travel industry? Will most people put financial decisions on hold until the extent of the war and its costs to the American tax payer is determined? Is the psychological effect so devastating and the outcome so uncertain that consumer confidence, and the free spending that accompanies it, will go into the toilet and flush the economy down with it?

The worst-case scenario is that the above questions all have "yes" for answers. Probably reality is somewhere between where things were at the beginning of September 2001 and our darkest fears. The reality for those over 50 is that their financial resources instantly got smaller. This loss, and the loss of our sense of well-being, which comes from being violated, coupled with the fear of possible future attacks, became a wake up call for most 50+ Boomers.

They've Got a New Attitude

The party's over. This doesn't mean that they'll stop being consumers. The recent political events mean that the Boomers will probably be making more considered purchases. They'll be smarter shoppers like in the late 80s and early 90s. Look for price brands and plain wraps to emerge again, gas consumption to become a concern, and vacations to be in the continental limits of the country rather than abroad. Look for a re-birth of "cocooning" as bringing family and friends together at home becomes more important. And look for a spiritual revival as a confused populace turns to a higher power for answers and direction.

The 50+ Boomers have not totally changed their characteristics of the "Me" generation or the overall playing field in which they operate. However, the perceived amount of time left on the scoreboard clock has changed. So, those who were planning for their future will be rethinking their game plan and those who were putting it off will start to seriously consider their options. And those who did not have a clue will remain that way. Unfortunately, there are still plenty of Boomers who still hope, if not believe, there's a pot of gold at the end of the rainbow. They think that when all is said and done, the government will magically find a way to take care of them because that's the way it's supposed to be. That's strange thinking for people who didn't trust the government 30 or so years ago. The sad thing is someone—their children, the government or both—will have to pay for them if they are unable to do it themselves.

Just as there was a marked increase in the sales of home-security systems and firearms following episodes of civil unrest in our cities in the past century, the sale of home, business and industrial security systems will flourish over the next several years, as will military and cybertech spending. This may provide the Cutting-Edge Boomers with investment opportunities to replace the recent dot com craze and fortify portions of the high-tech sector. Once the needs are identified for this "grave new world" in which we live, the financial resources will quickly follow to jump-start some areas of the market. Nobody likes to take points off the scoreboard, and many Cutting-Edge Boomers are looking for short-term returns since this could be the last time they'll be willing to be aggressive in the market. If you have a product or service designed to solve problems resulting from the declared war on terrorism, the 50+ Boomer is the right investment target for you.

Consumers staying home more will open up the high resolution TV, DVD, and digital recording (like TIVO) product categories. DSL and other computer accessories and peripherals should also experience renewed interest. Family focuses such as digital and film photography, scrapbooks and photo albums, holiday celebrations and decorating, meals that bring everyone together and adult games will have a resurgence with the 50+ Boomer. Also, the vacation home or rental where everyone can be together will gain popularity as the Cutting-Edge Boomer faces the reality of the world in which they live and reaches out to bring the family together for more family-focused activities.

A new morality and renewed patriotism will change what the 50+ consumer reads and watches. Violence in films and video games will receive pressure from this group. Gratuitous sex and adult language on TV may meet with similar disapproval because the nation, led by the 50+ Boomers, appears to be going back to the values they grew up with.

This giant group, which has been too busy making and spending money to bond together for any particular cause, now has a situation requiring their help. People from their parent's generation can't do much except provide them with support and remind them about how they coped following the bombing of Pearl Harbor and fighting a World War. The young people may have to fight for the freedom, but they can't provide the wisdom to guide the nation through the campaigns to ultimate victory. Ironically, the children of the 60s, the anti-establishment, war protesters are exactly the ones needed to provide the moral compass, leadership and commitment to ensure this country does what's right and keeps doing it until the world is free once more.

The Boomers Will Lead in More Ways than Consumption

While traveling throughout the country in the aftermath of the tragic events of September 11, I came to the conclusion that the absolute answer to getting the United States (and ultimately the global economy) back on track is the 50+ Boomer. They're the ones we listen to, and the ones who have the power plus the financial ability to effect change. Many of the 50+ Boomers have done an about face on the war issue. Some feel guilty about their lack of support for the fighting men and women, as manifested in their vehement opposition to the Vietnam War. The wounds have healed but the raw nerves are just below the surface. Others are simply frightened, never believing that things so horrible could happen here.

Many of the people influencing and making the decisions that will affect the lives of all Americans are the 50+ Boomers themselves, including George W. Bush, the president of the United States. As a result, more people will see through the thought, word and deed of how this important group will guide America's recovery to normalcy.

In the meantime, this same group of Cutting-Edge Boomers is prepared to show all of us the way out of the malaise. In fact, the movement has already begun. Many are recommitting to show the confidence they have in America because they know that the business of this country is business. They know that two-thirds of our Gross National Product (GNP) is a direct result of consumerism. They know that the way to beat terrorism, build confidence throughout the country, and get people back to work is by spending. However, the commitment of every American is

required so that we all succeed. The people who must be the catalyst that drives us to this victory are the marketing men and
women who have read this book.

You are the ones who can develop the products and services, fashion the strategies and inspire the creative implementation that will reach the 50+ Boomer and cause them to act. Once
they do, others will follow. Don't misdirect your efforts. Those
who are retired won't take the risks necessary to jump-start the
economy. The younger people are in a state of shock because they
never have been personally exposed to a war before. The Trailing
Boomers have children, mortgages, careers and other financial
distractions that keep them from being the driving force behind
the need to act, and act now.

Marketers must rethink the ways of appealing to the consumer in this post-tragedy era. Remember that we are talking
about the "Me" generation; they want to do something good for
themselves and to feel good while making others feel good too.

Even though many months have passed since September11,
the world is still in turmoil. People are looking for permission to
start buying again. It's necessary to spend money during these difficult times; those who do will be doing us all a favor. So your ad
messages must reflect this kind of attitude and you must direct
your communication efforts where they will do the most good:
towards the 50+ Boomer.

Chapter 19

It's Time to Profit from the 50+ Boomer

The notion that 50+ Boomers are setting the pace for those following them is hardly a startling concept. After all, they were the ones who established the tone for changing an entire generation back in the 60s. The Trailing Boomers merely followed their older brothers and sisters, wanting their piece of the pie, but not demonstrating the originality and courage of those preceding them. The Cutting-Edge Boomers clearly were, and still are, the leaders of their generation.

I see no reason for them to relinquish this powerful position and the control that goes with it. It's reasonable to assume that the Cutting-Edge Boomers will continue to be at the head of the parade and thereby influence all of the 76 million Boomers. However, their sphere of influence extends well beyond this important segment of the population.

The obvious immediate influence is exerted on those just ahead of them: those in their late 50s and early 60s. These people represent an important group of consumers too. The 50+ Boomers have kept those who preceded them young at heart while their older counterparts showed them how to grow up personally as well as professionally. In many ways, it's difficult to separate the actions of these long-standing compatible age groups. The result is a frontline of consumers that encompasses the important years leading up to the time when, in the past, most people were about to retire.

Of course, this accentuates the need to separate your marketing approach from the 18 to 49 or 25 to 54 demographic groups. They are just too broad of an age span and advertisers tend to direct their messages against the trailing, rather than the leading, ages of these segments. Nielsen now has a little used target of 35 to 64. Why this breakout is ignored by ad agencies is obvious; what TV shows appeal to a 35 year old and a 64 year old? Remember that there wasn't any show in the top 10 most viewed by those under 50 that made the list for those over 50.

A better breakout would be 50 to 64, 65 to 79, then 80+. Even though these breakouts aren't offered, extrapolating the data now will give you a leg up on the competition and help you to be better prepared as future strategies are developed. The 50-64 year old group currently represents more than 40 million consumers and that's a big group worth thinking about!

The behavioral difference between the oldest consumer and the youngest consumer in a 15 to 20 year audience segment is greater with younger groups, and these differences narrow as the cells increase in age. This does not suggest that the older people become more homogeneous in terms of behavior. Rather, it means that they exercise the experience they've gained and they don't particularly follow the lead of those in younger age groups.

Do you remember the big TV programming news story during the beginning of 2002? It was the possibility of David Letterman moving his late-night comedy show from CBS to ABC, which would replace the highly acclaimed *Night Line* news program hosted by Ted Koppel. Although Koppel had higher ratings, his average viewer age was 50+ while Letterman's smaller audience average age was in the mid 40s. As a result, ad agencies were willing to pay more money to reach fewer people. When this book went to print, it appeared that the tempest had subsided. Dave and Ted will stay put for the time being. However, a message has been sent to the 50+ consumer: You're not very important to those in the advertising business.

So why do marketers continue to ignore them, or try to motivate them with the wrong messages, or utilize the wrong media to reach this vital and growing core of consumers? I believe that, for the most part, it's a matter of negative conditioning about what influence age has on the marketing of goods and services. We've operated under the beliefs for many years that younger consumers are (1) the early adopters; (2) are more likely to switch brands; (3) are the heavy users; (4) are responsive to advertising; and (5) are generally big spenders. Well, it's time to challenge this archaic thinking.

I contacted nearly 50 of the country's leading marketers during the writing of this book. The purpose was to get examples of successful programs that they developed for the 50+ Boomers. The firms I contacted ranged from auto manufacturers to airlines, hotels to restaurant chains, supermarkets to Realtors, car rentals to cruise ships, pharmaceuticals to computer marketers, packaged goods to financial and service organizations. With a few notable exceptions, none of these firms could point to any program specifically targeted to the 50+ Boomer and most seemed to overlook them completely.

This kind of apathy is simply arrogant ignorance. The bright light is that some open-minded marketers are going to aggressively pursue the 50+ Boomer and lay claim to this potential gold mine. In many categories, minor brands will capture a major share of this waiting market. Are you going to own a disproportionately large share of the 50+ market and keep growing with it, or are you going to sit by until it becomes the fashionable thing to do?

If I accomplish anything with this book, I will have gotten you to the point where you are starting to question the status quo of traditional age profiling and the false ceilings that could restrict your product or service from reaching its true potential. Now that you're looking at the new opportunities offered by the 50+ Boomers, maybe it's time to encourage the other people on your marketing team to get on the same page with you. This means getting everyone involved in marketing, from the top down, including your advertising agency.

Start Riding the Wave Today

You might start by having a group meeting and asking them about the 50+ Boomers. Ask your team what Boomers mean to the business and what are the strategies being employed to capture them. I submit that you will find the answers less than satisfactory. Have them read this book as a starting point, and then schedule another group meeting and let them know you'll be asking the same questions. I promise you the answers will be more to your liking.

Why stop there? Select someone—maybe it's you—to be the company advocate for the 50+ Boomer segment of your business. Don't be surprised at how small this business may be initially or that you can't break out the information needed to quantify the 50+ Boomer's contribution to your bottom line. If you can't build the Cutting-Edge Boomer strategy from the inside out, do it from the outside in.

Start by reading everything you can about the subject of aging, from Gail Sheehy's *Passages* to Ken Dychtwald's *Age Wave*. There are also several other books dealing with marketing to older consumers. However, none that I've seen target the 50+ Boomer exclusively, so you'll have to interpret the information and draw your own conclusions as to whether the Cutting-Edge

Boomer is the consumer you want to know more about and determine the best ways to reach them. Be sure to read through past or current newsletters and syndicated research information to gain a better understanding of this potential market segment. Scouring through the information will yield tidbits that can give you a better understanding of this consumer or some insight about their needs, wants and desires. You'll also find loads of material in magazines such as *Modern Maturity* or general news periodicals like *Newsweek*. The food and home magazines also touch on the subjects as do newspapers. Consider the media that the 50+ Boomer is reading, viewing, or listening to, and you'll get a feel for the editorial and program formats, which appeal to this audience.

You might do what I've found helpful and go to the places where the 50+ Boomers go and talk with them. I meet them in retail stores, malls, and restaurants (no, I don't conduct table hopping research, but I will look for opportunities to talk while waiting for a table or to place my order). I also watch how they order and note the items they select. Other conducive venues are banks, the dentist or doctor's office, airports, supermarkets, parking lots—you name it and it's probably a place where I've engaged people in conversations that have helped me understand them better. And don't forget your friends who are 50+; with them you've got a ready-made informal focus groups. My wife thinks that I get a bit carried away with this activity, but I find it an extremely useful way to learn about what people are thinking and test reactions to a whole host of premises and concepts.

Mother-in law research, horseback surveys and information gathered on an informal or anecdotal basis is hardly a substitute for proprietary studies conducted by the pros. It would be presumptuous of me to suggest what kind of research would be best for you or who should conduct it. There are many qualified research organizations throughout this country. Participating in shared research projects such as those conducted by Nation Family Opinion (NFO) or developing an exclusive study by mail, phone, online, or personal intercept surveys can provide valuable, projectable data to help you make important business decisions. There are noted research firms such as the venerable Yankolovich organization, or smaller yet highly qualified groups scattered throughout the country. There's probably someone in your area who can provide the quantitative research capabilities you might need, your ad agency will know, and if you work for an agency, you're certainly working with such research firms already.

A good way to get in depth, diagnostic, qualitative information is through the use of the focus group technique. These groups usually consist of 10 to 12 people from your target audience who spend an hour and a half to two hours discussing predetermined subjects about products, services, current usage, and new concepts all under the direction of a qualified moderator. Usually a facility is used where you and key associates can see and hear the goings on while seated behind a one-way mirror. Usually several group sessions are held in a variety of cities to give clients a better feel for geographic differences in the consumers' reactions. I like the focus group form for gathering meaningful input, however the information is not projectable. It's usually the step to take on the way to developing a questionnaire before conducting quantitative research. This can arm you with vital insights in a matter of days or weeks if a number of sessions are conducted, versus possibly months for large projectable projects. Again, there are qualified firms in most major metropolitan markets. You or your agency should know of talented professionals specializing in this particular area of research.

Selfishly, I'd recommend that you call in a consultant, such as me, to help you get a fast "read" on the 50+ Boomer, develop a preliminary strategy to build a Boomer business and to start you on the road to forming a meaningful relationship with the Cutting-Edge Boomers. This relationship will be one that's designed to last for years to come. Short of that, immerse yourself, or the one designated by you, in all the aspects of knowing these 50+ consumers and learn how to communicate with them as well as what it takes to motivate them. Get your agency excited about the opportunities and if you're an agency person, take the lead and help your client get up to speed on the 50+ Boomer before someone else does.

Become a Boomer Advocate

Now, go about the process of digging for the facts and feelings about the 50+ Boomer. Match that with your current product or service mix, your distribution scheme and ultimately your overall marketing and advertising plans. Then go after this new and exciting segment for all it's worth—and it's worth plenty. Establish your brand with the 50+ Boomer, nurture them and take good care of them, and they'll respond by taking good care of you. As the number of 50+ Boomers continues to grow, your franchise with them can become stronger and your sales and profits will increase.

While you're becoming your company's expert on the 50+ Boomer and how to market to them, be sure to bring some of your younger people into the process, perhaps a representative in their early 40s and possibly another around 30. These people shouldn't be the point person on the 50+ Boomer project, but they can get a first-hand understanding of what this targeted consumer is all about. They can learn about the similarities and differences of the Cutting-Edge Boomers in comparison with your other important audiences. This information could help make believers of your younger marketing people just as I have tried to make one of you. Because knowledge is power, these people may develop some passion for the opportunities the 50+ Boomer offers to marketers who are in tune with them. Maybe they'll march to the beat of a new drummer. Maybe they'll understand that the 50+ Boomer is leading the marketing parade for now and in the foreseeable future.

Epilogue

Over the past several years, I have written and spoken to many people about the importance of the Cutting-Edge Boomers. I've discussed the importance of focusing on the 50+ segment because they have proven to be the leaders of this 76 million strong group, which is emerging and evolving in so many ways. From conventions and trade shows, to conferences and seminars to sales meeting and marketing symposiums, I have carried the torch and hopefully carried the message about the vitality of the 50+ Boomer as individuals and as consumers.

I wrote this book because it was a way to reach more marketers than through my past efforts and to help them become aware of the opportunities they may be missing. It was a way to raise the intellectual curiosity of a few brave souls with the courage and the instinct to really think strategically, rather than just look for new tactics to apply to the same consumer they have been reaching.

To that end, I will gladly answer your written, email or phone questions about what I may have learned about the 50+ Boomer. Furthermore, I would be honored to speak at an industry or company function, write an article, or meet with you and your marketing team to explore opportunities unique to your company. You can reach me as follows:

Don Potter
11300 Weddington Street, North Hollywood, CA 91602
Tel. (818) 760-8787 Ext. 102, Fax (818) 760-7756
Email: don@pkpf.net